GEORGE ELIOT

Her Mind and Her Art

GEORGE ELIOT

Her Mind and Her Art

BY

JOAN BENNETT

CAMBRIDGE
AT THE UNIVERSITY PRESS
1954

PUBLISHED BY
THE SYNDICS OF THE CAMBRIDGE UNIVERSITY PRESS

London Office: Bentley House, N.W. 1
American Branch: New York

Agents for Canada, India, and Pakistan: Macmillan

First Edition 1948
Reprinted 1954

Printed in Great Britain at the University Press, Cambridge
(Brooke Crutchley, University Printer)

To

RALPH WRIGHT

"Tous ceux dont nous sommes les débiteurs spirituels
accompagnent notre pensée à travers toutes ces opérations."

CHARLES DU BOS

CONTENTS

PREFACE

This book was already in the press when Mr Gerald Bullett's *George Eliot: Her Life and Books* was published. Mr Bullett takes account, as I have done, of the new biographical material in Dr A. T. Kitchel's *George Lewes and George Eliot*, and in Professor G. S. Haight's *George Eliot and John Chapman*; I do not believe, however, that his book makes mine redundant, since my approach to the subject is rather different. I am not attempting to write a new biography of George Eliot; the biographical first part of my book is meant only as an introduction to the second which examines her art as a novelist: I am only concerned with her life-story in so far as it is relevant to her work, so that I confine my attention to the development of her mind and personality prior to the inception of *Amos Barton* in 1856.

George Eliot's conversion from Evangelical Christianity to religious agnosticism and her illegal union with George Henry Lewes have been assumed, from her own time onward, to have affected her work. My belief is that neither event has been fully understood by most of her critics, either in its nature or in its bearings. The usual view is that her work suffered from both, because both caused her lasting distress of mind and therefore accentuated her preoccupation with moral questions, to the detriment of her creative power. An investigation of the evidence in contemporary sources of how she reached her intellectual conclusions, and of how she and Lewes arrived at their decision to live together may dispel certain prejudices which have affected the estimate of her work. It seems to me, at any rate, to throw some light on the relation between the creative artist and the intellectual woman in her. In the second part of this book I first describe the general characteristics of her art and attempt to show how the width of her knowledge and the strenuousness of her thinking contributed unobtrusively to the solidity and wisdom of the vision of life revealed in the novels. In subsequent chapters I consider the individual novels, not always in their entirety, but in some aspect that I have found especially interesting.

In her own lifetime George Eliot was widely acclaimed as the greatest of the English novelists, but it was, in the main, her earlier novels that were admired. Within ten years of her death her reputation steeply declined and by 1895, in *Corrected Impressions*, George Saintsbury wrote: 'For some years past George Eliot, though she may still be read, has more or less passed out of contemporary critical appreciation.' Sir Leslie Stephen in his *George Eliot* ('English Men of Letters', 1902), accepted the current view that a decline in her powers set in after *Romola*; that opinion was endorsed by W. J. Dawson in *The Makers of English Fiction*, 1905, where he states that 'For a period of four years in her life George Eliot wrote with consummate art. *Romola* marks her decadence...in *Middlemarch* this decadence is still more pronounced, and it is complete in the utterly tedious *Daniel Deronda*.' The revival of her reputation coincided with a change of view about the relative merits of her novels; in 1925 Virginia Woolf wrote in *The Common Reader*: 'It is not that her power diminishes, for, to our thinking, it is at its highest in *Middlemarch*, the magnificent book which, with all its imperfections, is one of the few English novels written for grown-up people.' From then onward George Eliot's reputation has risen; *Middlemarch* has been accepted as her masterpiece, while some critics have seen evidence of even greater creative power in parts of *Daniel Deronda* and of *Felix Holt*.[1] Some aspects of the modern estimate were anticipated by R. H. Hutton,[2] who had always admired her work and criticized it with insight, despite his opinion that her lack of religious faith clouded her vision with melancholy. He was

[1] See, for example, 'The Novels of George Eliot' by S. L. Bethell, *The Criterion*, 1938 and 'George Eliot' by F. R. Leavis, *Scrutiny*, 1945–6.
[2] R. H. Hutton, *Essays on some Modern Guides of English Thought*, 1887.

PREFACE

almost alone in 1885 in preferring *Middlemarch* to all her other
novels. Henry James, in other ways a forerunner of the modern
critics, continued to prefer the early works.[1]

The view I myself have reached, of which this book is the
product, is that there is no English novelist who has more to
offer the modern reader and that, despite the high excellence of
her novels preceding *Romola*, it is the later works that appeal
to us especially. George Eliot strikes us as one who 'writes
for grown-up people' because, unlike many of her contemporaries, she was not distracted from the contemplation of her
subject by the wish to provide the sort of entertainment the
reader demanded, nor by the wish to propagate specific views.
She concentrated on discovering all the bearings of the situations she invented. If she turns aside to lecture the reader
(a contemporary fashion to which she more often succumbed
in her early than in her later work), it is, nevertheless, in the
story itself and in the behaviour of the people who enact it that
her view of life reveals itself. Moreover, the asides are addressed
to adults; they assume that the reader has been attending and is
capable of co-operating with the author to understand the
human situation presented in the novel. A further effect of her
concentration on her subject is that her novels have organic
form, whereas serial publication and the magazine-reader's
demand for incident tended to produce episodic novels held
together by plot. Paradoxically, George Eliot's comparative
indifference to the amusement of the reader, or to his conversion
to this or that opinion, has endowed us with novels even more
entertaining and persuasive than those of any other Victorian
novelist. Furthermore, these novels invite and reward the
attention of the modern reader because George Eliot had faced
a problem which especially confronts the twentieth century: the
problem of how to preserve valuable moral attitudes which were
once closely associated with dogma. Although her rationalism

[1] Henry James, *Atlantic Monthly*, 1866, vol. XVIII, pp. 479–92; *Partial
Portraits*, 1888 (containing a review of Cross, first published in *Atlantic Monthly*,
1885, vol. LV, pp. 668–78).

is never explicit in the novels, yet it implicitly controls her vision of life. The point of view from which she contemplates the human situation reveals both her keen appreciation of traditional beliefs and customs and her own conviction that the substructure of dogma cannot endure; she is, however, in no doubt that the values it formerly sustained can survive it.

The first three of Professor Gordon S. Haight's six-volume edition of George Eliot's letters reached me when this reprint was already completed. His edition will double the number of letters and extracts from the journal previously printed, as well as restoring the text that J. W. Cross sometimes doctored. It includes also letters to and about George Eliot. The new material does not substantially alter my impression of George Eliot's intellectual and emotional development before she became a novelist, but Professor Haight's volumes will be indispensable for any future biographer, and are full of interest for all readers of George Eliot.

My debts to printed books, especially to biographies and memoirs of George Eliot's contemporaries, will be apparent in the text and in the bibliography. What I owe to the co-operation of my husband and to conversations with friends is less obvious and more pervasive. To one of these friends my book is dedicated; another, Mr George Rylands, gave valuable advice while the book was in manuscript. Whatever are its present shortcomings, they would have been greater but for his critical insight and his wide knowledge of the Victorian period.

THE FACTS

I. CHRONOLOGY

The facts are well known. One writes that and then remembers how easily facts slip out of the mind; therefore, in case some may be unknown and others forgotten, here are a few bare, but not always unimportant, facts.

1819. Mary Ann Evans born at Arbury Farm in Warwickshire. Her father Robert Evans, builder and carpenter like his father before him, became the estate agent of Francis Newdigate. In 1801 he had married Harriott Poynton and had two children by her. She died in 1809. In 1813 he married Christiana Pearson by whom he had three children, Christiana (b. 1814), Isaac (b. 1816) and Mary Ann (b. 22 Nov.).

1820. The second family moved from Arbury to Griff, an old red-brick house on the Arbury estate.

1824. Mary Ann was sent to boarding-school with Christiana at Attleborough, Warwickshire.

1828. Both sisters were transferred to a larger school at Nuneaton at which the 'principal governess' was Miss Lewis.

1832. Mary Ann was sent to a school at Coventry kept by the Misses Franklin, daughters of a Baptist minister.

1835. She was brought home because of her mother's illness.

1836. Her mother died.

1837. Christiana married and Mary Ann took charge of her father's household. While performing household duties (which included baking and jam making), and social duties (which included organizing a clothing club), she also studied Italian, German, Greek and Latin with the help of visiting teachers.

1839. Her Methodist aunt, Elizabeth Evans visited Griff. (She is also known as Mrs Samuel Evans and she told the story that suggested Hetty Sorrel in *Adam Bede*.)

1841. Isaac married and took over Griff.

1841. Robert Evans and Mary Ann moved to a house on the Foleshill Road, near Coventry. Here she formed a friendship with Charles Bray, a prosperous ribbon manufacturer, living at 'Rosehill', Coventry, the author of *The Philosophy of Necessity*; also with his brother-in-law Charles Hennell, author of *Inquiry Concerning the Origin of Christianity*, and with Charles's sister, Sara Hennell.

1842. Mary Ann decided that her present beliefs were incompatible with church attendance. Her father refused to live with her unless she conformed. She contemplated earning her living as a teacher. In the meanwhile she went to stay with her brother Isaac at Griff. After three weeks at Griff a reconciliation with her father was effected, she agreed to attend church and returned to Coventry.

1843. Miss Brabant married Charles Hennell and handed over to Mary Ann the task of translating Strauss's *Leben Jesu* on which she had been engaged.

1846. Publication of Strauss's *Life of Jesus*.

1849. Death of Robert Evans. Mary Ann inherited a small income for life. She travelled on the continent and stayed for some months in Switzerland.

1850. Returned to England. Stayed with the Brays for sixteen months. Contributed an article on Mackay's *Progress of the Intellect* to *The Westminster Review*.

1851. Marian (as she now began to be called) became assistant editor of *The Westminster Review* and boarded in the Strand with the editor, John Chapman, his wife and other lodgers. Here she formed a friendship with the rationalist philosopher, Herbert Spencer. He introduced her to George Henry Lewes.

1853. She moved to Cambridge Street and gave up her editorial work. She translated Feuerbach's *Essence of Christianity*, which was published under her own name in 1854.

1854. She went to Weimar with G. H. Lewes with whom she lived until his death in 1878.

1855. She returned to England with Lewes and lived at Richmond for three years.

1856. She wrote *Amos Barton* and began *Mr Gilfil's Love Story*.

1857. She wrote *Janet's Repentance*.

1858. The three stories, previously published in *Blackwood's Magazine*, were published together as *Scenes of Clerical Life* under the pen-name 'George Eliot'.

1859. She and Lewes moved to Holly Lodge, Wandsworth. Published *Adam Bede* and *The Lifted Veil*.

1860. *The Mill on the Floss* published. Visited Italy.

1861. *Silas Marner* published. Began *Romola*. Moved to Blandford Square.

1862. The first part of *Romola* published in *The Cornhill Magazine*.

1863. *Romola* completed. Moved to The Priory, Regent's Park.

1864. *Brother Jacob* published.

1866. *Felix Holt* published.

1867. Went to Spain, engaged in writing a blank-verse narrative, *The Spanish Gypsy*.

1868. *The Spanish Gypsy* published.

1869. Began another blank-verse story, *The Legend of Jubal*, published, 1874. *Middlemarch* begun.

1871. First part of *Middlemarch* published; the whole was finished by August 1872.

1872. *Middlemarch* published.

1876. *Daniel Deronda* published. Bought a house at Witley, Surrey.

1878. Wrote a series of Essays called *Impressions of Theophrastus Such*. 28 November, Lewes died.

1879. *Theophrastus Such* published.

1880. Married J. W. Cross in May. Moved from Witley to 4 Cheyne Walk, Chelsea, 3 December. Died 22 December.

II. WORKS

(a) NOVELS

1858. *Scenes of Clerical Life*. 2 vols. Edinburgh. [*Blackwood's Magazine*, Jan.–Nov. 1857.]

1859. *Adam Bede*. 3 vols. Edinburgh.

1860. *The Mill on the Floss*. 3 vols. Edinburgh.

1861. *Silas Marner: the Weaver of Raveloe*. Edinburgh.

1863. *Romola*. 3 vols. [*Cornhill Magazine*, July 1862—Aug. 1863.]

1866. *Felix Holt the Radical.* 3 vols. Edinburgh.
1871–2. *Middlemarch, a Study of Provincial Life.* 4 vols. Edinburgh.
1876. *Daniel Deronda.* 4 vols. Edinburgh.

(b) SHORT STORIES

1859. *The Lifted Veil.* [*Blackwood's Magazine*, July.]
1864. *Brother Jacob.* [*Cornhill Magazine*, July.]

(c) TRANSLATIONS AND ESSAYS

1846. *The Life of Jesus critically examined.* By D. F. Strauss.
1854. *The Essence of Christianity.* By L. Feuerbach. Trans. by Marian Evans.
1879. *Impressions of Theophrastus Such.* Edinburgh.

(d) POEMS

1868. *The Spanish Gypsy, a Poem.* Edinburgh.
1874. *The Legend of Jubal and other Poems.* Edinburgh.

Part I

The Formative Years:
Intellectual and Emotional
Development

CHAPTER I

BEFORE THE MOVE TO COVENTRY

WHEN HENRY JAMES tells us, in *The Middle Years*, of his brief but intimate encounter with George Eliot he declares that the personal contact added something for him to the enjoyment of her books, more particularly those he read afterwards:

> I found it intimately concerned in my perusal of *Middlemarch*, so soon then to appear, and even in that of *Deronda*, its intervention on behalf of which defied any chill of time.

Those two great works, the masterpiece and the failure alike, command the attention of any reader who delights in good fiction; but perhaps something would be added if we could establish a relation with the author:

> So it was, at any rate [Henry James continues], that my *relation*—for I didn't go so far as to call it ours—helped me to squeeze further values from the intrinsic substance of the copious final productions I have named, a weight of variety, dignity and beauty of which I have never allowed my measure to shrink.

He dictated those sentences in 1914 when, for most people, the measure of appreciation for George Eliot, and especially for her later work was shrinking. Since then it has expanded again; but it may be that if we could establish a closer relation with the author our appreciation of her work would be more discriminating and more complete than it is. The facts of her life are well known but they are easily misinterpreted; it is often supposed, for instance, that she shed her religious faith with equal ease and suddenness when she met the Hennells and the Brays at Coventry; and that the 'melancholy' in her books is the consequence of her unadmitted hankering for her lost religious beliefs. Or it is supposed that she lived to regret a hasty decision to live with

G. H. Lewes in spite of legal impediments and that she longed afterwards for the status of a married woman, which she achieved by her marriage with J. W. Cross, eighteen months after Lewes's death. When we look more closely at her own *Letters and Journals*[1] or at contemporary memoirs, neither of these suppositions remains credible. We are forced to discard the imaginary portrait of a frustrated woman, deprived by her own choices of religious support and of social dignity and consequently sternly preoccupied with the importance of morals. The caricature was never easily compatible with the impression of opulent power made by the novels. A perusal of printed evidences is a poor substitute for such an encounter as Henry James had when he found George Eliot deeply agitated by the illness of Lewes's son and was himself privileged to go and hasten the arrival of the doctor. But printed evidences are the only clue we have to the character of the author. From them we can learn much about the development of her thought and feeling prior to her creative activity. She was born with the gifts that made her a great novelist, but their development was slow and impeded and their idiosyncrasy is the consequence of nurture as well as nature.

It is possible to supplement our knowledge of the youthful Mary Ann Evans from the portraits of George Eliot's heroines Maggie Tulliver, Dorothea Brooke and, with certain added cautions, Romola. Of these three heroines, Maggie is the nearest to her author in circumstances, but all three have important intellectual and temperamental characteristics in common with her. They share her intense moral earnestness, her passionate nature with its tendency to self-mistrust and self-mortification, her thirst for

> large draughts of intellectual day

as well as

> thirsts of love more large than they.

And love for them all meant the opportunity for self-devotion as well as the assurance of being beloved. Like them also she

---

[1] J. W. Cross, *George Eliot's Life, Letters and Journals*.

suffered (until she found her own vocation) from the narrowness of the opportunities in her day for a young woman to develop and use intellectual powers. Mary Ann Evans would have welcomed such a suitor as Casaubon with the same feelings as did Dorothea. She may indeed have felt something similar (allowing for the different circumstances) for Dr Brabant when he handed over to her the wearisome task of translating Strauss's *Leben Jesu*. She was as ready as Dorothea to accept the scholar at his own valuation and to find joy in devoted service to his illusory grandeur of mind and soul.

But to understand her enthusiasm for the iconoclastic scholar we have first to watch the passionately religious little girl developing into the agnostic young woman. Religious zeal was not inculcated at home. All that we know about her father Robert Evans, and all that we guess when we attempt to make a composite picture from our impressions of Adam Bede, Mr Tulliver and Caleb Garth, assure us that it was not. Our right to use those three characters to help us derives in the first case from her own admission that Adam was 'suggested by my father's early life';[1] in the second from the fact that Maggie Tulliver is in a measure a self-portrait; and in the third from the fact that Caleb was, like Robert Evans, an estates manager of peculiar intelligence, integrity and devotion to his calling.[2] Of the three it is probably Caleb who most resembles Robert; whereas Tulliver has little in common with him except his relations with his wife's sisters and the quality of his love for his daughter. None of them is religious in the sense in which Mary Ann became religious under the influence of her schoolteacher Miss Lewis. It did not worry Robert that his daughter had become a Calvinist with a stern belief in predestination and a horror of all worldly delights. If it had he would not have sent her, after eight years at her evangelical school, to spend the next three under the Misses Franklin, daughters of a Baptist minister. Regular church

[1] Cross, vol. II, p. 67.
[2] Also Cross, doubtless with her authority, indicates that Caleb as well as Adam derived in a measure from Robert Evans.

attendance mattered to him as did all the orderly traditions of the English countryside. He was conservative rather than religious and was content with outward conformity and a high standard of moral conduct: 'a Tory who had not exactly a dislike for dissenters, but a slight opinion of them as persons of un-founded self-confidence'.[1] It was at her second boarding-school, of which Miss Lewis was principal and to which Mary Ann was sent with her elder sister at the age of eight, that she met for the first time with religious enthusiasm, a creed dominating the whole life and compelling self-repression and self-devotion. Moral earnestness and intellectual consistency were both native to her and she eagerly adopted the religious outlook of her teachers which dominated her life up to the age of twenty. Maggie Tulliver's masochistic self-repression is largely autobiographical. This is borne out by Mary Ann's letters to Miss Lewis. The first of those published by Cross was written when she was nineteen and records her first visit to London:

Let me tell you, though, that I was not at all delighted with the stir of the great Babel.

And no wonder since her brother Isaac remembered that 'she was so under the influence of religious and ascetic ideas, that she would not go to any of the theatres, but spent all her evenings alone reading'. In the same letter she writes:

For my part, when I hear of the marrying and giving in marriage that is constantly being transacted, I can only sigh for those who are multi-plying earthly ties which, though powerful enough to detach their hearts and thoughts from heaven, are so brittle as to be liable to be snapped asunder by every breeze....I must believe that those are the happiest who are not fermenting themselves by engaging in projects for earthly bliss, who are considering this life merely as a pilgrimage, a scene calling for diligence and watchfulness, not for repose and amusement. I do not deny that there may be many who can partake with a high degree of zest of all the lawful enjoyments the world can offer, and yet live in near communion with their God...but I confess

[1] Cross, vol. I, p. 4.

that in my short experience and narrow sphere of action I have never been able to attain to this. I find, as Dr Johnson said respecting his wine, total abstinence much easier than moderation. I do not wonder you are pleased with Pascal; his thoughts may be returned to again and again with increasing rather than diminished relish. I have highly enjoyed Hannah More's letters: the contemplation of so blessed a character as hers is very salutary.... Oh that we could live only for eternity! that we could realize its nearness! I know you do not love quotations, so I will not give you one; but if you do not distinctly remember it, do turn to the passage in Young's *Infidel Reclaimed* beginning, 'O vain, vain, vain all else eternity', and do love the lines for my sake.[1]

It is an odd and rather repellent letter from a girl of nineteen; but, with Maggie Tulliver to help us, it is not impossible to feel sympathy for the inexperienced, ardent girl who finds total self-repression easier than moderation. Single-minded devotion to a person or an idea remained her characteristic after she adopted a more liberal outlook, but neither Hannah More nor the poet Young were to retain her respect.

She wrote of the former in 1845 to John Sibree:

I am glad you detest Mrs Hannah More's letters. I like neither her letters, nor her books, nor her character;

while the latter is the subject of a devastating piece of criticism contributed by her to *The Westminster Review*, January 1857:

If it were not for the prospect of immortality, he considers, it would be wise and agreeable to be indecent, or to murder one's father; and, heaven apart, it would be extremely irrational in any man not to be a knave.

The same moral passion that attracted her to Young when she was a girl repels her when she is a woman. His insistence on immortality is mercenary:

...to us it is conceivable that in some minds the deep pathos lying in the thought of human mortality... lies nearer to the fountains of moral emotion than the conception of extended existence. And surely it

[1] Cross, vol. 1, p. 40.

ought to be a welcome fact if the conception of *mortality* as well as of immortality be favourable to virtue. Do writers of sermons and religious novels prefer that men should be vicious in order that there may be a more evident political and social necessity for printed sermons and clerical fictions? Because learned gentlemen are theological, are we to have no more simple honesty and good-will?

True virtue, she has discovered, flowers naturally out of good feeling, it has nothing to do with calculation; she draws an interesting parallel between morality and the arts:

On its theoretic and preceptive side, morality touches science; on its emotional side Art. Now, the products of Art are great in proportion as they result from that immediate prompting of innate power which we call genius, and not from laboured obedience to a theory or rule; and the presence of genius or innate prompting is directly opposed to the perpetual consciousness of a rule. The action of faculty is imperious, and excludes the reflection *why* it should act. In the same way in proportion as morality is emotional, that is has affinity with Art, it will exhibit itself in direct sympathetic feeling and action, and not as the recognition of a rule. Love does not say 'I ought to love'— it loves. Pity does not say 'It is right to be pitiful'—it pities. Justice does not say, 'I am bound to be just'—it feels justly. It is only where moral emotion is comparatively weak that the contemplation of a rule or theory habitually mingles with its action; and in accordance with this, we think experience, both in literature and life, has shown that the minds which are pre-eminently didactic— which insist on a 'lesson', and despise everything that will not convey a moral—are deficient in sympathetic emotion.

When George Eliot's heart and mind matured she came to believe that repression was not the surest road to virtue. In the meanwhile, her moral passion took an ascetic form, under the influence of her ardent affection for her teacher. Throughout the formative years we can observe two characteristics of the personality which was to develop into the genius of the novelist: the passionate force of her affections and the intellectual energy with which she pursues the inquiries those affections suggest to her. When her emotions are involved her first impulse is to embrace the creed of the person she loves. She has the artist's and the woman's impulse to identify herself with the object of her sympathies. But she has also a powerful intellect and a hunger of the mind which impel her to explore ideas and to retain and interconnect them. Both characteristics directed her towards the change of faith which was consummated at Coventry in 1841. A letter to Miss Lewis on 20 May 1839 expresses a recognition in herself of a tendency towards what Keats calls 'negative capability'. It can be set beside Keats's letter to Richard Woodhouse, 27 October 1818, about the 'poetical character'; Keats writes that:

A poet is the most unpoetical of anything in existence, because he has no identity.... It is a wretched thing to have to confess; but it is a very fact that not one word I utter can be taken for granted as an opinion growing out of my identical nature—how can it, when I have no nature? When I am in a room with people...the identity of everyone in the room begins to press upon me so that I am in a very little time annihilated....

Later, September 1819, Keats writes:

The only means of strengthening one's intellect is to make up one's mind about nothing—to let the mind be a thoroughfare for all thoughts.

For Mary Ann Evans, in 1839, there was a conflict between her need for intellectual clarity and integrity and the artist's impulse to sympathize and assimilate. She writes to Miss Lewis:

I think no one finds more difficulty in coming to a decision on controverted matters than myself. I do not mean that I have not preferences; but, however congruous a theory may be with my notions, I cannot find that comfortable repose that others appear to possess after having made their election of a class of sentiments. The other day Montaigne's motto came to my mind (it is mentioned by Pascal) as an appropriate one for me—'Que sais-je?'—beneath a pair of balances....

She is immediately aware of the dangers, to a devout Christian, of adopting such a motto and she adds:

...though, it is an ambiguous one, and may be taken in a sense that I desire to reprobate, as well as in a Scriptural one to which I do not refer. I use it in a limited sense as a representation of my oscillating judgment.

9

The views between which her judgement was oscillating at that time were those of the Evangelical Church and those of the Oxford Movement. Miss Lewis's devotion to the one and Isaac's conversion to the other must have divided her sympathies, and her intellect began to explore in both directions. The letter makes it clear that she has been focussing her attention upon two points at issue between them: first, the question of scriptural authority for episcopalianism and the ensuing controversy about the national establishment; and secondly, the fundamental doctrinal question about 'justification by faith'. She has been reading the works of writers on both sides:

On no subject do I veer to all points of the compass more frequently than on the nature of the visible Church. I am powerfully attracted in a certain direction, but when I am about to settle there, counter-assertions shake me from my position.... I have been reading the new prize essay on *Schism* by Professor Hoppus and Milner's *Church History* since I last wrote to you: the former ably expresses the tenets of those who deny that any form of Church government is so clearly dictated in Scripture as to possess a divine right, and, consequently, to be binding on Christians; the latter, you know, exhibits the views of a modern Evangelical Episcopalian on the inferences to be drawn from ecclesiastical remains.

Apparently these inferences are that separatists must not be excluded from 'the visible Church' but that episcopalianism and a national church are indicated as the best form of church government. She has also been reading Gresley's *Portrait of an English Churchman*, which seems to her to make extravagant claims for the superiority of the Anglican over all other Christian Churches, and the Oxford Tracts which

...evince by their compliments to Rome...and their attempts to give a Romish colour to our ordinance, with a very confused and unscriptural statement of the great doctrine of justification, a disposition rather to fraternise with the members of a Church carrying on her brow the prophetical epithets applied by St John to the Scarlet Beast, the mystery of iniquity, than with pious Nonconformists.

It is clear that, despite her love for her brother, Mary Ann's disposition is rather to 'fraternize' with the Nonconformists than with Rome. The protestant influence of Miss Lewis, an Evangelical churchwoman, had been followed up by the protestant influence of the Misses Franklin, who were Baptists. All these teachers, who had won her love and her respect, accepted Calvin's doctrine of election and of justification by faith. The doctrine teaches that good works cannot earn grace though they will be among the proofs that it has been given. In 1837 Mary Ann had been so convinced a Calvinist that she was shocked by the Arminianism of her Methodist aunt, her father's sister-in-law, the prototype of Dinah Morris. Mathilde Blind quotes, in her biography of George Eliot, from a letter written to Sara Hennell in 1859:

I had never talked with a Wesleyan before and we used to have little debates about predestination, for I was then a strong Calvinist. Here her superiority came out, and I remember now, with loving admiration, one thing which at the time I disapproved; it was not strictly a consequence of her Arminian belief, and at first sight might seem opposed to it, yet it came from the spirit of love which clings to the bad logic of Arminianism. When my Uncle came to fetch her, after she had been with us a fortnight or three weeks, he was speaking of a deceased minister, once greatly respected, who, from the action of trouble upon him had taken to small tippling, though otherwise not culpable. 'But I hope the good man is in heaven for all that', said my Uncle. 'Oh yes,' said my Aunt, with a deep inward groan of joyful conviction, 'Mr A's in heaven, that's sure.' This was at the time an offence to my stern, ascetic, hard views—how beautiful it is to me now.

It is interesting to notice here, in passing, that the anecdote of a good man who took to 'small tippling' as the result of 'trouble' was probably the germ of the short story *Janet's Repentance*.

The beliefs George Eliot held when she wrote that letter were gradually evolved during these early years (not suddenly adopted when she met the Brays in 1841). They were evolved by means of the books she read and thought about and to which she was led partly by her affections. If she differed in religious opinion from, for instance, her brother, it was necessary to her to explore the grounds of difference. Much of her reading in the years between 1839 and 1841 was governed by an interest thus awakened in the Oxford Movement. She was taking in much other mental nutriment as well: the poets, Latin grammar, mathematics, chemistry and metaphysics and she was uneasily aware that the evangelical dogmas to which she still clung were being put to some strain:

My mind presents...an assemblage of disjointed specimens of history ancient and modern; scraps of poetry picked up from Shake-speare, Cowper, Wordsworth, and Milton; morsels of Addison and Bacon, Latin verbs, geometry, entomology, and chemistry; Reviews and metaphysics,—all arrested and petrified and smothered by the fast thickening everyday accession of actual events, relative anxieties, and household cares and vexations. How deplorably and unaccountably evanescent are our frames of mind, as various as the forms and hues of the summer clouds! A single word is sometimes enough to give an entirely new mould to our thoughts—at least I find myself so consti-tuted; and therefore to me it is pre-eminently important to be anchored within the veil, so that outward things may be unable to send me adrift.

This was written to Miss Lewis on 4 September 1839 (at the close of her twentieth year). In her next letter she is beginning to learn German. Equally relevant to the impending change in her outlook, she is pursuing her inquiries into the history of the Church. She is engaged in making a chart of ecclesiastical history, begun a year earlier and abandoned a year later when one was published 'far superior to mine in design'. In May 1840 she tells Miss Lewis that she has been enjoying Keble's *Christian Year* and that she is about to read *The Oxford Tracts* and *Lyra Apostolica*, 'the former I almost shrink from the labour of conning'. The study of Italian, the reading of Spenser's *Faerie Queene*, then of Mrs Somerville's *Connection of the Physical Sciences*, as well as her household duties (including 'boiling currant-jelly') may have delayed her approach to the *Tracts*; but by August she had read them as well as a long, careful, erudite book of controversy against the Puseyites, Isaac Taylor's *Ancient*

Christianity and The Oxford Tracts. Of this book Mrs Cash of Coventry wrote: 'From the impression made on my own mind by unfavourable facts about "The Fathers" and from her own subsequent references to this work, I am inclined to think it had its influence in unsettling her views of Christianity.' All that Mary Ann Evans herself says about the book to Miss Lewis on 12 August 1840 is that she has been reading St Paul's Epistle to the Colossians in connection with a train of thought suggested by it. She notes particularly Paul's warning in the Epistle against 'the beggarly elements of a spirit of self-righteousness'. The parts of the Epistle she has in mind are doubtless these:

Let no man therefore judge you in meat, or in drink, or in respect of a feast day or a new moon or a sabbath day: which are a shadow of the things to come; but the body is Christ's....If ye died with Christ from the rudiments of the world, why, as though living in the world, do ye subject yourselves to ordinances? Handle not, nor taste, nor touch (all which things are to perish with the using), after the precepts and doctrines of men? Which things have indeed a show of wisdom in will-worship, and humility, and severity to the body; but are not of any value against the indulgence of the flesh.

And upon this follow St Paul's admonitions to restrain themselves from 'fornication, uncleanness, passion, evil desire, and covetousness' and to cultivate 'compassion, kindness, humility, meekness, long-suffering; forbearing one another, and forgiving each other...and above all these things put on love, which is the bond of perfectness'. After which St Paul gives special counsels of mutual forbearance to husbands, wives, children and servants. The letter to Miss Lewis says:

I have been reading it in connection with a train of thought suggested by the reading of *Ancient Christianity and The Oxford Tracts* by Isaac Taylor, one of the most eloquent, acute, and pious of writers. Five numbers only have yet appeared. Have you seen them? If not I should like to send you an abstract of his argument. I have gulped it (pardon my coarseness) in a most reptile-like fashion. I must *chew* it thoroughly to facilitate its assimilation with my mental frame.

The three main points which would be bound to remain in her mind after 'gulping' and still more after 'chewing' Isaac Taylor's book, are these: first, the relevance of the study of the origins of Christianity and the early history of the Church to the formulation of her own beliefs; secondly, the moral dangers of any extreme asceticism; thirdly, the necessity to apply common sense and a knowledge of the law of consequences to religious beliefs. These three considerations eventually led her to humanistic rationalism.

The writers of *The Oxford Tracts* believed that pure Christianity flourished in the third and fourth centuries before Rome acquired supremacy over the Church. Taylor wrote his book to prove that all the corruptions that Protestants associate with the Roman Supremacy were already rife in the third century. The deduction he intends to make is that pure Gospel Christianity must be sought in the Gospels themselves and that the renewed endeavour made at the Reformation to discover and rely on those sources must be continued. To establish his point he examines the records of the early Church. John Henry Newman, exploring the same ground in 1839, which is the year in which Taylor published his attack on the *Tracts*, came to the conclusion that the decisions made in Rome in reference to the various heretical doctrines that arose in the fifth century were invariably right. It was this discovery that led him on towards Roman Catholicism. In the *Apologia Pro Vita Sua* he tells us that in the course of the Long Vacation, 1839, he was studying the history of the Monophysites:

It was during this course of reading that for the first time a doubt came upon me of the tenableness of Anglicanism....My stronghold was Antiquity; now here, in the middle of the fifth century, I found, as it seemed to me, Christendom of the sixteenth and the nineteenth centuries reflected. I saw my face in that mirror, and I was a Monophysite.

Newman finds that the early Church bred a number of heresies, comparable to the post-Reformation heresies of the Protestant sects, including opinions still sanctioned by the Established Church of England. And he finds that what he believes to be the just definitions of doctrines (such as the true nature of Christ defined in controversy with Monophysites) were owing to the decisions of Rome. Thus Newman, examining Antiquity, finds it wanting and consequently becomes a Roman Catholic. At the same time Isaac Taylor looks at Antiquity, finds it wanting and adheres to Evangelical Protestantism. Mary Ann Evans follows the direction in which he points and, ultimately, abandons all theological dogma. But, whereas Newman's attention was focussed, characteristically, upon theological controversies in the early Church, Taylor's attention and Mary Ann Evans's were, equally characteristically, focussed mainly on the moral doctrine and practice of the early Church.

On one point Newman and Taylor are agreed. Both believe that the Roman domination effected an improvement in the early Church. But Taylor thinks that this improvement still fell far short of the primitive purity of Gospel Christianity to which the reformed Churches must constantly look. He writes that:

Particular points had in view, it might be affirmed that Popery was a practicable form, and corrected expression of Ancient Christianity;

and again that:

Popery, foul as it is and has ever been, might yet fairly represent itself as a reform upon early Christianity.

This is a part of his argument against the Oxford Movement; and a similar view of the early Church, to which that movement turned as the source of the true faith, led Newman to abandon Anglicanism. But, for Taylor, Romanism perpetuates the radical error of the early Church, namely its exaltation of the celibate and the ascetic:

This artificial purity was then a violent reaction, ending, as might have been foreseen, and as every convulsive moral struggle must, in a correspondent corruption, as well of manners as of principles.

This is his most insistent argument against the early Church and it is obvious that it would cause Mary Ann Evans to reflect seriously upon her own ethical opinions. Only a year before she had written

. . . when I hear of the marrying and giving in marriage that is constantly being transacted, I can only sigh. . . .

and now this 'most eloquent, acute, and pious of writers' shows her that the attempt to exalt a code of behaviour antagonistic to human nature was perverse and that

. . . the sentiments of real virtue were so broken in upon, by this pernicious system of factitious and superhuman piety, that the sexes could no longer be suffered, with any safety, ever to live together under the same roof.

Taylor affirms that:

The fundamental principles and practices of religious celibacy were at once the product and the indication of certain notions concerning the Divine Nature altogether unlike those conveyed in the Scriptures, and which took effect upon every other element of Ancient Christianity.

He asserts that, although the Catholic Church pronounced against the Gnostic heresy, yet

. . . at a very early period, it yielded itself to the undefined and more seductive gnostic principle, which made the conditions of animal life, and the common alliances of man in the social system, the antithesis of the divine perfections, and so to be escaped from, and decried, by all who panted after the highest excellence.

This abhorrence of 'the conditions of animal life' and this dread of 'the common alliances of man in the social system' had hitherto been part of Mary Ann Evans's own attitude to life, as they were later to be part of Maggie Tulliver's creed, under the influence of Thomas à Kempis. Mary Ann 'saw her face in that mirror' and she was a gnostic, or perhaps a Manichean. At least she began to suspect that she had been wrong. Moreover, Taylor gives her a clue with which to solve moral problems:

'*Let the same mind be in you as was in Christ Jesus who pleased not himself.*' This sovereign rule of behaviour may make a man a martyr, or may induce him to lead a single life, or may impel him to traverse the globe having no certain dwelling place—when the doing so shall clearly, and in the judgment of good sense, tend to promote truth in the world.

Mary Ann Evans was soon to accept the view that self-repression was not a good in itself, but only as it served some discernible end; that is, for her, only as it promoted the welfare of others.

But Isaac Taylor's book, besides making her revise some of her ethical assumptions, must also have given her an impulse towards research into the origins of Christianity. Taylor poses very clearly the question at issue between Protestantism and Catholicism, the question whether the full Christian Gospel and doctrine can be found in Scripture, or whether it is to be gradually evolved in the Church:

Was Christianity complete and mature in the hands of the Apostles, or was it then in bud merely, waiting to be ripened by the suns and showers of many centuries? If we assume the former position, and reject altogether Tertullian's doctrine, then we must not only reject Popery and its usurpations, but the immemorial errors also of Ancient Christianity.

This question about the source of her faith led her energetic and inquiring mind to explore by every available means into the origins of Christianity. Before she met the Brays at Coventry she had already read *An Inquiry concerning the Origin of Christianity* by Charles Bray's brother-in-law, Charles Hennell. Isaac Taylor's book would naturally have directed her to it and would have prepared her to accept its approach to the subject, for Taylor writes:

As everyone knows that, in order to acquire a genuine acquaintance with history, we must examine the extant original materials of the times in question; so everyone knows, that these contemporary materials are to be examined in the full light of our *modern* good sense and general intelligence.

Thus Mary Ann Evans, driven because of her love on the one hand for her brother and on the other for Miss Lewis, to explore the points at issue between Puseyites and Evangelicals, took the first step which eventually led her to abandon all dogmatic religious beliefs.

CHAPTER II

COVENTRY

IN 1841 Isaac Evans married and took over the Evans's home at Griff. In March 1841 Mary Ann and her father moved to a house on the Foleshill Road, near Coventry. This house was next door to that of Mrs Pears, a sister of Charles Bray with whom the Evans family were already slightly acquainted. In May the Evanses and the Brays met at Mrs Pears's house. Apparently it was not until the following November that Miss Evans visited the Brays' house[1] it is uncertain where and how often the two families had met in the intervening months; but Charles Bray's autobiography[2] describes a quickly ripening friendship between them:

Although I had known Mary Ann Evans as a child at her father's house at Griff, our real acquaintance began in 1841, after she came with her father to reside near Coventry, my sister, who lived next door to her, thinking, amongst other natural reasons for introducing her, that the influence of this superior young lady of Evangelical principles might be beneficial to our heretical minds. She was then about one and twenty, and I can well recollect her appearance and modest demeanour as she sat down on a low ottoman by the window, and I had a sort of surprised feeling when she first spoke, at the measured, highly cultivated mode of expression, so different from the usual tones of young persons from the country. We became friends at once. We soon found that her mind was already turning towards greater freedom of thought in religious opinion, that she had even bought for herself Hennell's *Inquiry* and there was much mutual interest between the author and herself in their frequent meetings at our house.

In a footnote, Bray quotes from a letter to Sara Hennell written by Mary Ann Evans in 1847:

I have read the *Inquiry* again with more than interest,—with delight and high admiration. My present impression from it far surpasses the

[1] Cross, vol. I, p. 92.   [2] *Phases of Opinion and Experience during a Long Life.*

one I had retained from my two readings about five years ago. Apart from any opinion of the book as an explanation of the existence of Christianity and the Christian documents I am sure that no one fitted to read it at all could read it without being intellectually and morally stronger—the reasoning is so close, the induction so clever, the style so clear, vigorous and pointed, and the animus so candid and even generous.

From what Bray writes and from this quotation it seems clear that Miss Evans had read *An Inquiry* before she was reintroduced to the Brays. The 'two readings about five years ago' would then be actually six years before she wrote this letter; presumably one reading before she met the Brays and discussed such matters with them and one after. The dates are not important in themselves but it is of importance to establish the fact that there was no sudden *volte-face* at Coventry. The popular view, that she shed her Christianity overnight and that she visited the Brays hoping to convert them, but was instead converted by them, does not accord with the impression of her mind derived from her writings. She was neither unthoughtful nor arrogant. What seems actually to have happened is that she pursued a course of reading which led gradually to an increasing scepticism about the grounds of her belief. She read Hennell's *Inquiry* in natural sequence to Isaac Taylor's *Ancient Christianity*. Moreover, with regard to what happened at Coventry it is also necessary to take into account the two characteristics of her nature, not only her intellectual curiosity, but also her dependence on the affections. She was persuaded by the rationalistic arguments of her friends; she was persuaded the more readily because of the mutual liking that sprang up between her and them. From childhood both mind and heart inclined her to embrace the opinions of the people she liked. It seemed to her logical as well as emotionally satisfying to suppose that those whose lives she approved of thought justly. In 1840 she wrote to Miss Lewis:

I remember, as I daresay you do, a very amiable atheist depicted by Bulwer in *Devereux*; and for some time after the perusal of that book, which I read seven or eight years ago, I was considerably shaken by the impression that religion was not requisite to moral excellence.

She must then have read *Devereux* when she was twelve or thirteen years old. At Coventry, at the age of twenty-two, she met the same phenomenon in real life and at a moment when her intellectual assurance of her Evangelical beliefs was already wavering. Bray records that she said 'Mr Hennell seemed to me a model of moral excellence'. The facts about how Hennell came to write *An Inquiry* suggest that she was right. Both Hennell and Bray were excellent people, as can be discerned in the unselfconscious revelations of Bray's autobiography and in Hennell's book. Both had in a rare degree, intellectual honesty and moral courage.

Charles Bray was brought up as a Methodist; he did not, however, take religion seriously until, at the age of seventeen, he was converted by an Evangelical Dissenter. His conversion coincided with a breakdown in health, the result of overwork, and he spent three months at the seaside:

No three months of my life were happier than these, and to this not only the cessation from too hard work, but my new religious views greatly contributed; and they also enabled me to break away from bad habits, and to withstand temptation, as I am sure nothing else would have done.

He returned to London to work again at the warehouse at which he was articled, but the work proved too severe and he joined his father in his business at Coventry, at the age of nineteen (1830):

My religion was now my great delight; my sisters were also what is called 'Evangelical'.... In strict accordance with my opinions I avoided general society in a world to which I did not belong; to me it was 'the unclean thing'.

He had been a reader from his early boyhood but now he read nothing but religious books:

Gibbon and Hume were objects of my pity.... Naturally this attitude of mind engendered an immense amount of self-sufficiency and religious pride, which led to what many will regard as my fall, and which I look upon as my emancipation.

He attempted to convert the Unitarian minister 'an exceedingly
modest, intelligent and well-informed man', to his own Trinitarian
doctrine:

> I did not for a moment think that his worldly interests would stand
> in the way, any more than they would have done with myself.

There is no suggestion that this confidence was misplaced, but
the boy had met his match both in learning and in logic. The
minister countered his Scriptural proofs by comparing the
English Bible with the Vulgate and by enlightening him about
textual criticism:

> It became clear to me that if we had the 'Word of God' we required
> also an inspired translation, and more than that, since all the world
> interpreted differently, an inspired interpretation. Both of these the
> Romish Church profess to have, if you choose to take their word for it.

Charles Bray did not; he returned to his Bible-reading armed with
his newly discovered liberty of interpreting and with his native
good sense and sense of justice. Before long he found himself
unable to accept even as much Christian doctrine as do the
Unitarians:

> The next year was certainly the most miserable year of my life.
> I had given up my faith, and with it many of my dearest friends, and
> I had to begin to build my life over again; my mind was in a complete
> anarchy, or in a state of blank despair.

He emerged from this with the foundations of his permanent
beliefs firmly laid:

> I had one Truth about which I was certain, viz., that no part of the
> Creation had been left to chance, or what is called free-will; that the
> laws of mind were equally fixed or determined with those of matter,
> and that all instinct in beasts, and calculation in man, required that they
> should be so fixed. I set myself to work, therefore, gradually and
> laboriously, to build up a system of ethics in harmony with this
> established fact. I found that *everything* acted necessarily in accordance
> with its own nature, and that there was no freedom of choice beyond
> this; consequently, if there could be no virtue in the ordinary sense of
> that term, i.e., in action that is determined, neither could there be any

sin.... What then was virtue? Not that which is free, spontaneous or uncaused, but that which does the greatest amount of good, or produces most happiness.... We love that man best who, we know, *cannot*, from his *nature*, be a nasty sneak, or do a mean thing. We should be sorry to think he was *free* to be the one or to do the other.

From this nucleus he developed his *magnum opus*, *The Philosophy of Necessity*, published in 1841, the year before Mary Ann Evans joined the circle at Coventry. Ten years before this he had accidentally come across George Combe's *Phrenology* with its doctrine that the whole of a man's potential character can be deduced from the conformation of his head. This new 'science', which attracted many of the contemporary rationalists at least for a while (including Mary Ann Evans) was enthusiastically believed in by Bray from thenceforward, despite all the criticism of the theory that convinced men of wider scientific attainments, among whom was George Henry Lewes. Charles Bray was as hard-headed and obstinate as he was intellectually honest and courageous. Once a doctrine satisfied his common sense and his sense of justice and accorded with his limited experience, nothing would move him from it. Moreover, the rebuff he met with when he attempted to convert the Unitarian minister did not deter him from attempting to convert people to his new doctrines. He was as fervent a missionary for determinism and phrenology as he had once been for Evangelicalism. In 1836 he married and he himself tells us, with engaging good humour, how he set about converting his wife on the honeymoon. His wife was Charles Hennell's sister.

The same confidence in what then appeared to me to be the truth, which made me think I could convince the Unitarian Minister, made me now think that I had only to lay my new views on religious matters before my wife for her to accept them at once. Consequently I had provided myself with Mirabeau's *System of Nature*, Volney's *Ruins of Empire*, and other light reading of that sort to enliven the honeymoon. But again I was mistaken, and I only succeeded in making my wife exceedingly uncomfortable. She had been brought up in the Unitarian Faith, and, as might be expected in a young person of one-and-twenty, religion with her was not a question of theological controversy or Biblical criticism, but of deep feeling and cherished home associations, and of convictions instilled into her mind from childhood under the influence of one of the most cultivated and powerful Unitarian preachers of the day, the Rev. Robert Aspland. She ultimately referred the critical part of the matter to her elder brother, Charles, C. Hennell, who had already gone very fully into the subject, and had come out completely convinced on the Unitarian standpoints. He refused at first to reconsider the question, but, influenced more by my philosophical arguments—for I knew nothing of Biblical Criticism— he at length consented to investigate the evidence once more. The result of his study was Hennell's *Inquiry concerning the Origin of Christianity*, a work which had considerable influence as being one of the first attempts to regard Christianity from a purely historical point of view, and to analyse the life and work of its Founder in a reverent, truthful, and appreciative spirit, while separating from it all that was obviously legendary or mythical.

Whatever views one may hold about the controversial religious questions at issue, one cannot fail to admire the mental energy, the honesty and the courage of the people involved in this anecdote. After her brother's change of view Mrs Bray followed suit and she and her husband ceased to attend church. Bray writes that: 'This singularity has, I believe, interfered much with my utility in public life.' All of this throws light on the Coventry group with whom Mary Ann became intimate.

Bray gives a vivid and convincing portrait of what she was like at this time:

I saw a great deal of her, we had long frequent walks together, and I consider her the most delightful companion I have ever known; she knew everything. She had little self-assertion; her aim was always to show her friends off to advantage—not herself. She would polish up their witticisms, and give them the *full* credit of them. But there were two sides; hers was the temperament of genius which has always its sunny and shady sides. She was frequently very depressed—and often very provoking, as much so as she could be agreeable—and we had violent quarrels; but the next day, or whenever we met, they were quite forgotten, and no allusion made to them. Of course we went over all subjects in heaven or earth. We agreed in opinion pretty well at that time, and I may claim to have laid down the base of that philosophy which she afterwards retained.

One of her recent critics has stated that she held as a solemn conviction—the result of a lifetime of observation—that in proportion as the thoughts of men and women are removed from the earth on which they live, are diverted from their own mutual relations and responsibilities of which they alone know anything, to an invisible world, which can only be apprehended by belief, they are led to neglect their duty to each other, to squander their strength in vain speculations, which can result in no profit to themselves or their fellow-creatures, which diminish their capacity for strenuous and worthy action during a span of life, brief, indeed, but whose consequences will extend to remote posterity.[1]

Charles Bray adds that he himself already held these opinions in 1842 and implies that he laid the foundations of her belief. They were foundations well adapted to bear a structure of thought embracing the philosophy of Auguste Comte with which she was soon to become intimately acquainted.

Charles Bray has a right to claim his share among the influences which shaped George Eliot's vision of life. Their friendship ripened at the time when her Evangelical beliefs were ceasing to satisfy her; his brother-in-law's book gave her an acceptable account of the origins of those beliefs and Bray gave her an acceptable rationalization for her natural tendency to altruistic conduct. There was no subsequent revolution in her ideas; the standpoint of Herbert Spencer, of G. H. Lewes, of the writings of Auguste Comte and of Feuerbach tended to confirm and enlarge, not to alter, the conceptions she developed at Coventry.

Bray goes on to describe her temperament, apparently relying as much on phrenology (the reading of a cast of her head made in 1844) as on his own observations. Whatever the source of his opinions they are, in the main, confirmed by her biography:

She was of a most affectionate disposition, always requiring someone to lean upon, preferring what has hitherto been considered the stronger

[1] The reference is to *The Congregationalist*, April 1881.

sex, to the other and more impressible. She was not fitted to stand alone. Her sense of Character—of men and things, is a predominantly intellectual one, with which the Feelings have little to do, and the exceeding fairness, for which she is noted, towards all parties, towards all sects and denominations, is probably owing to her little feeling on the subject,—at least not enough to interfere with her judgment. She saw all sides, and they are always many, clearly and without prejudices.

Much of what Bray here writes of her temperament is borne out by the story of her life. 'She was not fitted to stand alone'; this is in one sense true and is confirmed by her letters and by her life. She depended upon reciprocated affection; and, although her intellect was masculine, her temperament was essentially feminine; also, as is common with intelligent women, she preferred 'the stronger sex'. From the Coventry period to the end of her life, though she had many close friendships with women, there was always at least one man with whom she was on intimate terms and who shared in her intellectual interests; Charles Bray, Charles Hennell, John Sibree and later Herbert Spencer, G. H. Lewes and Frederic Harrison were among the most worthy of her regard, while men with more specious gifts such as Dr Brabant and John Chapman were, for a time at least, over-estimated by her. Her 'exceeding fairness towards all parties' is apparent in her work; but Bray's explanation of it tells us more of himself than of her. It was not the result of 'little feeling on the subject' but rather of breadth of sympathy and understanding and of the creative artist's 'negative capability'. She had the power which she herself describes in a letter to John Sibree in 1848 where she writes:

Artistic power seems to me to resemble dramatic power—to be an intimate perception of the varied states of which the human mind is susceptible, with ability to give them out anew in intensified expression.

Unlike Bray himself and unlike her contemporary Harriet Martineau (another convert to positivism) she did not embrace new and congenial opinions with uncritical ardour; delight in a writer's vision of life was compatible for her with only a partial acceptance of his beliefs. Writing to Sara Hennell in February 1849 she says:

I wish you thoroughly to understand that the writers who have most profoundly influenced me—who have rolled away the waters from their bed, raised new mountains and spread delicious valleys for me—are not in the least oracles to me. It is just possible that I may not embrace one of their opinions.

She goes on to tell of the effect upon her of the writings of Rousseau who has

...so quickened my faculties that I have been able to shape more definitely for myself ideas which previously dwelt as dim *Ahnungen* in my soul; the fire of his genius has so fused together old thoughts and prejudices, that I have been ready to make new combinations.

and of George Sand; to whose morals Sara Hennell had evidently objected:

I should never dream of going to her as a moral code or text book. I don't care whether I agree with her about marriage or not—whether I think the design of her plot correct, or that she had no precise design at all, but began to write as the spirit moved her and trusted to Providence for the catastrophe, which I think the more probable case. It is sufficient for me, as a reason for bowing down before her in eternal gratitude to that 'great power of God manifested in her', that I cannot read six pages of hers without feeling that it is given to her to delineate human passion and its results and (I must say, in spite of your judgment) some of the moral instincts and their tendencies, with such truthfulness, such nicety of discrimination, such tragic power, and withal, such loving, gentle humour, that one might live a century with nothing but one's own dull faculties, and not know as much as six pages will suggest.

All the positives in this appreciation of George Sand's fiction are applicable to George Eliot's own.

On 13 November 1841, eleven days after her visit to the Brays' house, Mary Ann wrote to Miss Lewis and for the first time (if one may judge by the extracts given by Cross) gives her friend an intimation that her beliefs are changing:

> My whole soul has been engrossed in the most interesting of all inquiries for the last few days, and to what results my thoughts may lead, I know not—possibly to one that will startle you; but my only desire is to know the truth, my only fear to cling to error. I venture to say our love will not decompose under the influence of separation, unless you excommunicate me for differing from you in opinion. Think—is there any *conceivable* alteration in me that would prevent your coming to me at Christmas?

About three weeks later (8 December) the extract from her letter to Miss Lewis begins:

> What a pity that while mathematics are indubitable, immutable, and no one doubts the properties of a triangle or a circle, doctrines infinitely more important to man are buried in a charnel-heap of bones over which nothing is heard but the barks and growls of contention.

It does not seem possible to discover precisely how Miss Lewis bore the defection of her pupil and dear friend; but such evidence as there is speaks well for her. Presumably, she did pay the Christmas visit for, in 1875, George Eliot writes to Sara Hennell:

> I wonder if you all remember an old governess of mine who used to visit me at Foleshill—a Miss Lewis? I have found her out. She is living at Leamington, old, but cheerful, and so delighted to be remembered with gratitude. How very old we are all getting! But I hope you don't mind it any more than I do. One sees so many contemporaries, that one is well in fashion. The approach of parting is the bitterness of age.

The last extract Cross gives from a letter to Miss Lewis, written on 19 February 1842, incorporates the doctrine of Charles Bray and identifies it with the teaching of St Paul. It occurs after Mary Ann Evans has quoted some lines of her own composition:

> Beautiful ego-ism, to quote one's own. But where is not this same ego? The martyr at the stake seeks its gratification as much as the court sycophant, the difference lying in the comparative dignity and beauty

of the two egos. People absurdly talk of self-denial. Why, there is none in Virtue to a being of moral excellence: the greatest torture to such a soul would be to run counter to the dictates of conscience; to wallow in the slough of meanness, deception, revenge or sensuality. This was St Paul's idea in the 1st chapter of the 2nd Epistle to Timothy. (I think that is the passage.)

If her reference is correct she is presumably thinking of verses 7–9.

For God gave us not a spirit of fearfulness; but of power and love and discipline. Be not ashamed therefore of the testimony of our Lord, nor of me his prisoner; but suffer hardship with the gospel according to the power of God; who saved us, and called us with a holy calling, not according to our works, but according to his own purpose and grace, which was given us in Christ Jesus before times eternal.

Although it may be disingenuous to identify St Paul's doctrine of divine grace with rationalistic determinism it is not difficult to interpret the same facts of experience by either philosophy. A 'being of moral excellence' or one of God's chosen is equally incapable of 'wallowing in the slough of meanness'. That some human beings should be by nature more inclined to good than others may seem unjust when it is explained as the result of an arbitrary election by a Divine Being. It is true, nevertheless. The sense of injustice disappears when a personal deity, reserving rewards and punishments for his predestined creatures, is no longer assumed.

After nine months at Coventry (March to November 1841) Mary Ann had sufficiently made up her own mind to be ready to declare her change of view and to suffer the consequences. To a young woman of an ardently affectionate disposition they were by no means trifling. At first it seemed wrong to her to continue going to church and this decision deeply offended her father; he made church attendance the condition of his continuing to live with her. The house was put into the hands of agents; Mr Evans proposed to go and live with his married daughter and Mary Ann was to move into lodgings at Leamington and try to support herself by teaching. The letters give some indication of her suffering at this time and of the way her mind was working. The crisis came early in 1842; in January she writes to Mrs Bray:

I shall be most thankful for the opportunity of going to Leamington, and Mrs Pears is willing to go too. There is but *one* woe, that of leaving my dear father—all else, doleful lodgings, scanty meals and *gazing-stockism*, are quite indifferent to me. Therefore do not fear for me when I am once settled in my home—wherever it may be—and freed from wretched suspense.

A letter to Mrs Pears in the following month (the same month as the 'predestination' letter to Miss Lewis) shows how she was gradually moving away from the convert's dogmatism and proselytizing spirit towards that tolerance and sympathy which are characteristic of her maturity. The letter also gives a clear account of her release from Calvinism:

I can rejoice in all the joys of humanity,—in all that serves to elevate and purify feeling and action; nor will I quarrel with the million who, I am persuaded, are with me in intention, though our dialects differ. Of course I must desire the ultimate downfall of error, for no error is innocuous; but this assuredly will occur without my proselytising aid, and the best proof of a real love of the truth—that freshest stamp of divinity—is a calm confidence in its intrinsic power to secure its own high destiny,—that of universal empire. Do not fear that I will become a stagnant pool by a self-sufficient determination only to listen to my own echo; to read the yea, yea on my own side, and be most comfortably deaf to the nay, nay. Would that all rejected *practically* this maxim. To *fear* the examination of any proposition appears to me an intellectual and a moral palsy that will ever hinder the firm grasping of any substance whatever. For my part, I wish to be among the ranks of that glorious crusade that is seeking to set Truth's Holy Sepulchre free from a usurped domination. We shall then see her resurrection. Meanwhile, although I cannot rank among my principles of action a fear of vengeance eternal, gratitude for predestined salvation, or a revelation of future glories as a reward, I fully participate in the belief that the only heaven here, or hereafter, is to be found in conformity with the will of the Supreme; a continued aiming at the attainment of the perfect ideal, the true *Logos* that dwells in the bosom of the one

Father. I hardly know whether I am ranting after the fashion of one of the Primitive Methodist prophetesses, with a cart for her rostrum, I am writing so fast.

There is an element of 'rant' in the style of the letter, just as there is an element of her Methodist aunt's moral enthusiasm in her nature. In substance what she writes is a sound expression of the belief she now held; her moral certainties were unaffected by her change of doctrine. It appears that her father withdrew the house from the agent's hands; presumably her brother intervened, for Mary Ann went to stay with Mr and Mrs Isaac Evans at Griff. It is worth noting that Isaac was evidently not so narrow and hard-hearted a young man as Tom Tulliver who, because of his relation to Maggie, is usually assumed to represent him. It is obviously unwise to identify characters in the novels too precisely with characters in real life. Mary Ann writes to Mrs Pears from Griff (March 1842):

I have here in every way abundant and unlooked-for blessings— delicacy and consideration from all whom I have seen; and I really begin to recant my old belief about the indifference of all the world to me, for my acquaintances of this neighbourhood seem to seek an opportunity of smiling on me in spite of my heresy.

She is, in this letter, deeply disturbed about the breach with her father; she does not much expect him to relent and she does not seem as yet to have decided upon the compromise she sub- sequently made, although her affection for her father and her good sense are impelling her towards it:

On a retrospection of the past month, I regret nothing so much as my own impetuosity both of feeling and judging. I am not inclined to be sanguine as to my dear father's future determination, and I sometimes have an intensely vivid consciousness, which I only allow to be a fleeting one, of all that is painful and that has been so. I can only learn that my father has commenced his alterations at Packington, but he only appears to be temporarily acquiescing in my brother's advice 'not to be in a hurry'. I do not intend to remain here longer than three weeks, or, at the very farthest, a month; and if I am not then recalled,

I shall write for definite directions. I must have a *home*, not a visiting place. I wish you would learn something from my father and send me word how he seems disposed.

Mary Ann remained at Griff for three weeks, after which, Cross tells us, 'through the intervention of her brother, the Brays and Miss Rebecca Franklin' (her former teacher) 'the father was very glad to receive her again, and she resumed going to church as before'.

This was in April 1842, three months after the breach between father and daughter. A letter to Sara Hennell written eighteen months later, 19 October 1843, shows how she came to be able to conform with the practice of church attendance:

I will tell you, as briefly as possible, my present opinion, which you know is contrary to the one I held in the first instance. I am inclined to think that such a change of sentiment is likely to happen to most persons whose views on religious matters undergo a change early in life. The first impulse of a young and ingenuous mind is to withhold the slightest sanction from all that contains even a mixture of supposed error. When the soul is liberated from the wretched giant's bed of dogmas on which it has been racked and stretched ever since it began to think, there is a feeling of exultation and strong hope. We think we shall run well when we have the full use of our limbs and the bracing air of independence, and we believe that we shall soon obtain something positive which will not only more than compensate us for what we have renounced, but will be so well worth offering to others, that we may venture to proselytise as fast as our zeal for truth may prompt us. But a year or two of reflection, and the experience of our own miserable weakness, which will ill afford to part even with the crutch of superstition, must, I think, effect a change. Speculative truth begins to appear but a shadow of individual minds. Agreement between intellects seems unattainable, and we turn to the *truth of feeling* as the only universal bond of union. We find that the intellectual errors which we once fancied were a mere incrustation have grown into the living body, and that we cannot in the majority of cases wrench them away without destroying vitality. We begin to find that with individuals, as with nations, the only safe revolution is one arising out of the wants which their own progress has generated. It is the quackery of infidelity to suppose that it has a nostrum for all mankind, and to say to all and singular, 'Swallow my opinions and you shall be whole'. If, then, we are debarred by such considerations from trying to reorganise opinions, are we to remain aloof from our fellow-creatures on occasions when we may fully sympathise with the feelings exercised, although our own have been melted into another mould? Ought we not on every opportunity to seek to have our feelings in harmony, though not in union, with those who are often richer in the fruits of faith, though not in reason, than ourselves? The results of non-conformity in a family are just an epitome of what happens on a larger scale in the world. An influential member chooses to omit an observance which, in the minds of all the rest, is associated with what is highest and most venerable. He cannot make his reasons intelligible, and so his conduct is regarded as a relaxation of the hold that moral ties had on him previously. The rest are infected with the disease they imagine in him. All the screws by which order was maintained are loosened, and in more than one case a person's happiness may be ruined by the confusion of ideas which took the form of principles. But it may be said, how then are we to do anything towards the advancement of mankind? Are we to go on cherishing superstitions out of a fear that seems inconsistent with any faith in a Supreme Being? I think the best and the only way of fulfilling our mission is to sow good seed in good (i.e., prepared) ground, and not to root up tares where we must inevitably gather all the wheat with them. We cannot fight and struggle enough for freedom of inquiry, and we need not be idle in imparting all that is pure and lovely to children whose minds are unbespoken. Those who can write—let them do so as boldly as they like—and let no one hesitate at proper seasons to make a full confession (far better than profession). St Paul's reasoning about the conduct of the strong towards the weak, in the 14th and 15th chapters of Romans, is just in point.

This letter was written when Mary Ann was twenty-four; it indicates her rapid advance towards that imaginative understanding of human nature and that combination of reason and sympathy which inform the novels of George Eliot.

For the next six years, October 1843 until her father's death in May 1849, Mary Ann kept house for him at Foleshill. There was forbearance as well as devoted love on both sides. During these years her circle of friends expanded, largely owing to her intimacy with the Brays, and her intellectual horizon steadily widened. She seems at this time to have read with almost equal ease in Latin, in French, and in German. She went for holidays with the Brays and met at various times such acquaintances of theirs as Robert Owen, of whom she says:

I think if his system prosper it will be in spite of its founder, and not because of his advocacy;

and Harriet Martineau, with whom she was later to become more intimate. But the most important renewed or new personal relationships were those with the Sibrees and with the Brabants.

The Sibrees, like the Brays, were a Nonconformist family and they were friends of the Misses Franklin, to whose school Mary Ann had been sent at the age of twelve. The Sibrees' house was also on the Foleshill Road and Miss Franklin called to tell Mrs Sibree that 'an old pupil of whom she herself and her sister Rebecca had always been very proud' was coming to live within five minutes' walk of their house. Mrs Sibree looked forward to meeting the pious little girl who had made an impression in the neighbourhood in her school days. Mary Sibree, then a girl of sixteen, was able to supply some clear recollections to J. W. Cross when he was compiling *George Eliot's Life, Letters and Journals*. She recalls that:

Miss Franklin dwelt with much pride on Miss Evans' mental power, on her skill in music etc.; but the great recommendation to my mother's interest was the zeal for others which had marked her earnest piety at school, where she had induced the girls to come together for prayer, and which had led her to visit the poor most diligently in the cottages round her own home.[1]

Miss Evans, despite her changing religious views, was still ready to join in good works; she and Mrs Pears had started a clothing club for the neighbouring poor before her first visit to

[1] Cross, vol. 1, p. 156.

Mrs Sibree. When late in 1841, along with the rest of Mary Ann's circle, Mrs Sibree became aware of her change of views, she bore it well and the friendship continued. Mary Sibree gives a vivid impression of the sense of emancipation and renewed life that followed immediately upon Mary Ann's renunciation of dogma:

It was very evident at this time...that the desire for congenial society, as well as for books and larger opportunities for culture, which had led her most eagerly to seek a removal from Griff to a home near Coventry, had been met beyond her highest expectations. In Mr and Mrs Bray, and in the Hennell family, she had found friends who called forth her interest and stimulated her powers in no common degree. This was traceable even in externals,—in the changed tone of voice and manner—from formality to a geniality which opened my heart to her, and made the next five years the most important epoch of my life. She gave me (as yet in my teens) weekly lessons in German, speaking freely on all subjects, but with no attempt to directly unsettle my Evangelical beliefs, confining herself in these matters to a steady protest against the claim of the Evangelicals to an exclusive possession of higher motives to morality—or even to religion.[1]

When in 1843, apparently under the influence of her brother John, Mary Sibree herself began to waver in her Evangelical beliefs she went to Mary Ann Evans for help and sympathy. Miss Evans directed her attention away from the theoretical questions to an immediate question of practical morals. Mary Sibree was teaching arithmetic and her knowledge of it was far from thorough. Her friend advised her to get her conscience clear about that and also not to turn to her for advice 'until my views of religion were also clear'.

It was through her relation to Dr Brabant that Mary Ann Evans came to translate Strauss's *Leben Jesu*, the task that occupied her for the three years from 1844 to 1846. It may seem a far cry from that laborious task-work to the creative fiction which was to prove her vocation; it was, nevertheless, her apprenticeship to letters; moreover, quite apart from her critical interest in the matter of Strauss's book, she was fascinated by the

[1] Ibid. p. 158.

medium in which she worked, she was profoundly interested in words. Four years before she undertook this task, in 1840, when she was studying Italian, she wrote to Miss Lewis:

I fear I am laboriously doing nothing, for I am beguiled by the fascination that the study of languages has for my capricious mind. I could e'en give myself up to making discoveries in the world of words.

And during the progress of what she often found a heart-breaking task the search for exact verbal equivalents for the German beguiled her. It is possible that some other language or some less cumbersome work would have served her better. But, such as it was, the work of translating gave her her first experience of sustained writing.

Her relation to Dr Brabant is also interesting on other grounds. Cross tells us little about it, but something can be discovered through John Chapman's *Diary*, edited by Professor Gordon S. Haight, and through Eliza Lynn Linton's *My Literary Life in London*. Neither Chapman nor Mrs Lynn Linton is a trustworthy witness and both of them rely on what may have been the same secondary sources. Mrs Linton speaks of 'a family tradition' as her authority and Chapman hears the story he relates eight years after the events to which it refers. With due caution these accounts can, nevertheless, be used to supplement the facts recorded by Cross and the bare account in Charles Bray's autobiography of how Mary Ann Evans came to undertake the translation of Strauss. In July 1843 Mary Ann, the Brays, and Charles and Sara Hennell went for a holiday together accompanied by Dr Brabant and his daughter. At this time Miss Brabant had undertaken to translate Strauss's book. During the year, possibly on this holiday, she became engaged to Charles Hennell. The marriage took place on 1 November. Bray writes:

In November, 1843, we went to London to be present at Charles Hennell's marriage with Miss Brabant at Finsbury Chapel, where W. J. Fox, one of the most eloquent preachers of the day, was the officiating minister. Miss Evans went with us, and was one of the bridesmaids, and she afterwards paid a visit to Dr Brabant, the bride's father, at Devizes, in order to cheer him upon the loss of his only daughter. Dr Brabant was a personal friend of Dr Strauss and a profound German scholar, and under his direction, his daughter had begun to translate the 'Leben Jesu'. But after translating two chapters, her marriage interfering with the work, Miss Evans was persuaded by Mr Hennell to undertake the completion of it.

Cross does not mention Mary Ann's visit to the Brabants nor quote from the letters referring to it. Mrs Lynn Linton supplies a character sketch of Dr Brabant:

My first introduction to Bath and Walter Savage Landor was through Dr Brabant, a learned man who used up his literary energies in thought and desire to do rather than in actual doing, and whose fastidiousness made his work something like Penelope's web. Ever writing and re-writing, correcting and destroying, he never got further than the introductory chapter of a book which he intended to be epoch making, and the final destroyer of superstition and theological dogma.

By the way, Dr Brabant was one of the men whose undeniable attainments won the enthusiasm of George Eliot—then Mary Ann Evans. A family tradition chronicles a scene which took place between the young woman and the elderly man, when she knelt at his feet and offered to devote her life to his service. Between a wife who, though blind, counted for something in the councils of the household, and a vigilant sister-in-law who looked sharply after the interests of all concerned, this offer of a life-long devotion proved abortive. The enthusiasm of the girl was promptly stifled under the wet blanket thrown over it by an alarmed wife and a sister who thought such spiritual attachments might lead to danger; and Mary Ann Evans left the house a sadder woman than she entered it.

At this date Dr Brabant was about sixty-three years old and Mary Ann was twenty-four. The anecdote has, like most anecdotes, a measure of appropriateness to the characters involved. But all that Mrs Lynn Linton writes about George Eliot and about G. H. Lewes must be received with caution. She was too hasty and ardent in judgement to be reliable; as her friend and biographer Mr George Somes Layard writes: 'She was

a partisan to the back-bone, and had the strength—and weakness—of those who cannot see both sides of a question.' Her
warm friendship for Mrs G. H. Lewes and for Thornton Hunt
prejudiced her against Lewes and George Eliot. But this
does not affect the convincing likeness between her portrait of
Brabant and George Eliot's portrait of Casaubon in *Middlemarch*. Moreover, the ardent, half-deluded devotion of Mary
Ann to Dr Brabant is wholly consonant with her temperament
and the impression derived from Mrs Lynn Linton is supple-
mented by the other (though equally unreliable) source, John
Chapman's diary. Mary Ann was warned by Mrs Bray, Chapman
says, against Brabant and to the warning she replied:

He is a finer character than you think—beautifully sincere, conscientious and benevolent, and everything besides that one would have
one's friends to be.

With him she pursued her study of Greek; and, according to
the account which, so Chapman alleges, was given to him by
Brabant's daughter Rufa Hennell, in 1851

...in the simplicity of her heart and her ignorance of (or incapability of
practising) the required conventionalisms, gave the Doctor the utmost
attention; they became very intimate; his sister-in-law, Miss S. Hughes,
became alarmed, made a great stir, excited the jealousy of Mrs Brabant.
Miss Evans left. Mrs Brabant vowed she should never enter the house
again. Brabant's unmanliness in the affair was condemned more by
Mrs Hennell than by Miss Evans herself.

It is not easy to discern what precisely constituted the
'unmanliness' of Brabant, nor to decide just how much to
discount because of Chapman's propensity to scent a domestic
melodrama in any story involving relations between the sexes.
His own domestic arrangements, in which Mary Ann Evans later
became involved, were highly peculiar and his diary reveals a sex-
obsession which would be liable to distort his views. But,
allowing for all this, it is still possible to discover in the relation
between Mary Ann and Brabant the seed of George Eliot's
understanding of what Dorothea felt for Casaubon. Also the

diary and Mrs Linton between them supply an element in Mary Ann's character which is largely suppressed by Cross. She was, despite her keen intelligence and her well-disciplined mind, as much governed by her emotions as was her own Maggie Tulliver. Her need for affection and for an object for self-devotion is sometimes discernible even through the carefully expurgated letters Cross prints. There is, for instance, this passage in a letter to Mrs Pears, during the difficult period in Mary Ann's relation with her father, February 1842:

I was really touched that you should think of *me* while among friends more closely linked with you in every way. I was beginning to get used to the conviction that, ivy-like as I am by nature, I must (as we see ivy do sometimes) shoot out into an isolated tree;

or this unexplained paragraph in a letter to Sara Hennell, August 1845:

Your letter describes what I *have* felt rather than what I feel. It seems as if my affections were quietly sinking down to temperate, and I every day seem more and more to value thought rather than feeling. I do not think this is man's best estate, but it is better than what I have sometimes known.

Cross quotes a passage to the same correspondent, in April 1849, which even more clearly reveals her temperament and the drive which would ultimately transfer her energies to creative writing:

Tell me not that I am a mere prater—that feeling never talks. I will talk, and caress, and look lovingly, until death makes me as stony as the Gorgon-like heads of all the judicious people I know. What is anything worth until it is uttered? Is not the universe one great utterance? Utterance there must be in word and deed to make life of any worth.

In Mary Ann Evans's relation with Miss Lewis, in her relation with the Brays, the Hennells, the Sibrees and with Brabant the two sides of her nature are equally apparent, the intellectual energy and also the emotional ardour, the desire to know the truth and also to be absorbed into some devoted service. Both sides ultimately combined in the 'negative capability' or receptiveness, and the out-giving energy or need for utterance which formed the creative artist.

The translation of the *Leben Jesu* occupied her mind for three years during which she continued to keep house for her father and to be his devoted companion. The translation exhilarated her, exasperated her and bored her by turns. Her father was almost continuously ill and she herself suffered from nervous exhaustion. Mrs Bray writes to Sara Hennell:

Poor thing, I do pity her sometimes, with her pale sickly face and dreadful headaches, and anxiety too about her father. This illness of his has tried her so much, for all the time she had for rest and fresh air she had to read to him. Nevertheless she looks very happy and satisfied sometimes in her work.

At last, in April 1846, the translation was finished; it was published by John Chapman in June with a preface by Strauss and without the translator's name. Between 1843 and 1849 when her father died Mary Ann contributed occasional articles and reviews to *The Coventry Herald* which was edited by Charles Bray, including an anonymous review of J. A. Froude's *The Nemesis of Faith*. Apparently Froude recognized in the review the style of the translator of Strauss; he wrote to his reviewer, through John Chapman, begging that he might be told the name of the author. Cross does not tell us whether or no she revealed herself; but she showed Froude's letter with pleasure to the Brays and Mrs Bray wrote to Miss Hennell:

Poor girl, I am so pleased she should have this little episode in her dull life.

Her life, however, was not intellectually dull; in April she began to translate Spinoza's *Tractatus Theologico-Politicus*; Mrs Bray writes that:

M.A. is happy now with this Spinoza to do: she says it is such a rest for her mind.

It is noteworthy that she should have been studying Spinoza at this time; his work was as yet very little known in England. Coleridge and Shelley had rediscovered him, but their interest had not led them to translate his work nor to publish any comprehensive account of it; and, when G. H. Lewes wrote an essay on Spinoza for *The Westminster Review* in 1843, he claimed that it was 'the first attempt to vindicate the great philosopher before the English public', a claim which Frederick Pollock accepted in 1880 in his *Spinoza, his Life and Philosophy*. Lewes had been introduced to Spinoza's work in 1836: Mary Ann found the *Ethics* and the *Tractatus Theologico-Politicus* on Dr Brabant's shelves in the same year in which Lewes, as yet unknown to her, published his essay in the review she was later to edit. She abandoned her translation of the *Tractatus* after her father's death because, as she wrote to Charles Bray, she felt that:

What is wanted in English is not a translation of Spinoza's works but a true estimate of his life and system. After one has rendered the Latin faithfully into English, one feels that there is another yet more difficult process of translation for the reader to effect, and that the only mode of making Spinoza accessible to a larger number is to study his books, then shut them up and give an analysis.[1]

Presumably she felt the same when, in 1854, she abandoned, or, at least, refrained from publishing, her translation of the *Ethics*; a work far more difficult for the general reader to understand. With both works now available in English it is, however, not difficult to see why they appealed so strongly both to her and to Lewes. Spinoza felt, as they both did, that speculative theology was a subject for fruitless and unending dispute and one from which no profit could derive. He had read the Bible with the same scholarly attention as he would have given to any other book, taking full account of the time, as far as he could ascertain it, at which any part of it was written, of the people for whom it was written and of the language of the writers. The conclusions he puts forward in the *Tractatus* are similar in kind to those in Hennell's *Inquiry* and in Strauss's *Leben Jesu*; the records are

[1] Cross, vol. 1, p. 238.

human and fallible and the way in which doctrine is presented is adapted to the people for whom it was set down. The true religion which can be learnt from the Bible is the same religion as that to which man's reason leads him: 'How happy would our own age be, could we see religion freed from every kind of superstition.' And what Spinoza means by 'religion' is 'to love God above all, and our neighbour as ourselves'. Nor does he allow any mystery to accrue round the meaning of 'Love God above all', since he asserts that the Bible does not invite speculation about the nature of God. It only inculcates obedience: 'Now since obedience to God consists in the love of our neighbour...it follows that in Scripture no other science is recommended save that which is necessary to mankind, in order that by obeying God in conformity with the precept of neighbourly love they may show themselves obedient to him...,' or again 'most assuredly we are bound by Scriptures to believe nothing more than is necessary to carry out the divine command of Godly and neighbourly love'. Spinoza was the most distinguished among the thinkers who helped Mary Ann Evans to free herself from the 'Procrustean bed of dogma'. This freedom from any moral compulsion to believe the unintelligible she would derive from the *Tractatus*, while the *Ethics* would confirm her emancipation from the belief that self-denial is a good in itself. The girl who at twenty starved her own love of music and sighed to read of marriages was now ready to assent to Spinoza's proposition that 'Nothing but gloomy and sad superstition forbids enjoyment', and to welcome Spinoza's conception of virtue as its own reward. 'Blessedness is not the reward of virtue, but is virtue itself; nor do we delight in blessedness because we restrain our lusts; but, on the contrary, because we delight in it, therefore we are able to restrain them.'

Robert Evans died in May 1849 and with his death an epoch of his daughter's life ended. She was no longer tied to any one place nor constricted by any domestic duties. She had to make a new life for herself.

CHAPTER III

LONDON

WHEN her father died in May 1849 Mary Ann Evans was twenty-nine years old. She had given some of the best years of her life to the care of an ageing invalid and had found in this service a satisfaction for that side of her nature which craved for an object of self-devotion. Meanwhile, she had also found means to cultivate and to employ her vigorous intellect. But the death of her father at first seemed to leave her life empty of meaning and purpose. Moreover her health, which was never good, had suffered considerably from the strain of her father's last illness. Her tremendous emotional and intellectual energy was always liable to tax her physical constitution beyond its strength, and the letters both from Coventry and later from London refer frequently to violent headaches and other symptoms of nervous exhaustion. For the eight months following on her father's death she lived abroad and recuperated her strength. She went with the Brays to the continent for a month and they left her in a pension in Switzerland at Campagne Plongeon, from which she moved to Geneva where she stayed for five months in the congenial home of M. and Mme d'Albert Durade, who became her life-long friends. M. d'Albert Durade was later to translate the *Scenes of Clerical Life*, *Adam Bede*, *Silas Marner*, *Romola* and *Felix Holt* into French. The correspondence from Switzerland confirms and intensifies the impression already formed of her nature and temperament. Evidence accumulates of her passionate need to give and to receive affection, combined with an intellectual energy which, even at its lowest ebb and when impeded by ill-health, is extraordinary. She writes, for instance, to Charles Bray on 4 December 1849:

Spinoza and I have been divorced for several months. My want of health has obliged me to renounce all application. I take walks, play

43

the piano, read Voltaire, talk to my friends, and just take a dose of mathematics every day to prevent my brain from becoming quite soft.

In a letter to Mrs Bray on the same day we have a glimpse of the other side of her nature, the hunger for emotional out-giving which was drawing her back to England:

> My heart-ties are not loosened by distance—it is not in the nature of ties to be so; and when I think of my loved ones as those to whom I can be a comforter, a help, I long to be with them again. Otherwise I can only think with a shudder of returning to England. It looks to me like a land of gloom, of *ennui*, of platitude; but in the midst of all this it is the land of duty and affection, and the only ardent hope I have for my future life is to have given to me some woman's duty—some possibility of devoting myself where I may see a daily result of pure calm blessedness in the life of another.

More than four years were still to elapse before that hope was fulfilled and the urgency of her need for its fulfilment accounts for a measure of emotional instability in the years that intervened.

She returned to England in March 1850. Cross gives us very little insight into what happened between this date and July 1854, when she went to Weimar with George Henry Lewes in defiance of the marriage law. In fact, Cross's *George Eliot's Life, Letters and Journals*, invaluable for all that it includes, is in some respects dangerously misleading. Dangerously, because it creates an image sufficiently venerable to tempt the iconoclast. The creator of Janet Dempster, Maggie Tulliver, Mrs Transome and Gwendolen Harleth who, with deliberate recklessness, threw in her lot with G. H. Lewes, knew more about the passions, and especially about the passion of love, than appears in the carefully edited and expurgated letters and journals. Mrs Lynn Linton, who knew Marian Evans[1] in these early years in London and who was doubly envious of George Eliot, was the first to attempt iconoclasm. She was probably a little jealous of George Eliot's solid achievement as a rival novelist, although she acknowledges her rival's deserts; but she was explicitly jealous because George

---

[1] Mary Ann signed her translation of Strauss's *Leben Jesu* as Marian Evans and from that time she was known as Marian.

Eliot's breach with the conventions had been so generally condoned. When Cross's *Life* appeared she wrote a review in *Temple Bar*[1] sufficiently derogatory to the subject to provoke a letter from Herbert Spencer. In her reply she says of Lewes and George Eliot:

> There were people who worshipped these two, who cut me because I separated from Linton, and who would have held Thornton Hunt good for stoning. Mr Lewes and Miss Evans were perfectly justified in their union—perfectly—but they were not justified in their assumption of special sacredness, nor was the world in its attitude of special reverence, which was more than condonation. It is this sense of favouritism and consequent unfairness that has animated me in all that I have said.[2]

This sense of unfairness was natural; it was also liable to make her over-emphasize the other side of the picture and to discover for her readers any trait in George Eliot which seemed the reverse of noble. There is, however, no shocking revelation in the *Temple Bar* article, but there are indications of those aspects of character which Cross has somewhat obscured; for instance:

> Without sympathy from many her gifts of mind were of no avail and the love of one was essential to her very existence.

There is also a hint in Mrs Linton's letter to Herbert Spencer, of an earlier love episode with a man whom she had found peculiarly disagreeable. The reference is possibly to John Chapman. Certainly Professor Gordon S. Haight's edition of Chapman's *Diary* helps to fill out the account of these four years. There is, however, need to step warily in using it as evidence, because of the peculiar character of the diarist.

Chapman lived *en ménage* with his wife Susanna and his mistress, Elisabeth Tilley; in his diary he expresses surprise and even moral indignation when difficulties ensue. He professes an equal love to both women and perceives no inconvenience in increasing his commitments of this kind. Whatever actually happened, it is clear

---

[1] *Temple Bar*, 1885.
[2] George Somes Layard, *Mrs Lynn Linton. Her Life, Letters and Opinions*, p. 251.

that he attempted to establish a close intimacy with Mary Ann Evans. John Chapman may have supplied some aspects of Stephen Guest in *The Mill on the Floss*; he had in common with him at any rate coxcombry and good looks; Professor Haight reproduces a photograph, which shows him to have been a remarkably handsome man at the age of 69, and we are told that in youth he was nicknamed Byron because of his resemblance to the portraits of the poet. Besides his physical advantages and practised charm, Chapman had a potent spell to cast over Mary Ann in that he genuinely needed her co-operation. Chapman belonged to the same intellectual world as her friends the Brays and the Hennells and it was at his house that she met Herbert Spencer who later introduced her to Lewes. It must not of course be supposed that any of these men shared Chapman's peculiarly anarchistic notions about sexual relations; these were the result of his temperament rather than of the intellectual climate in which he lived.

When Marian returned to England, in March 1850, she went to the Brays at Rosehill for a few days and then for a few weeks to her brother at Griff. From there she wrote to Sara Hennell, 'Will you send me an account of Mr Chapman's prices for lodgers, and if you know anything of other boarding houses etc. in London'. She did not go to reside at the Chapmans until 8 January 1851; the intervening time was spent mainly at Rosehill. From there she contributed to *The Westminster Review* a review of Mackay's *Progress of the Intellect*. By the autumn Chapman was owner as well as editor of that paper. Cross tells us that Mackay and Chapman visited Rosehill in October 1850, 'and there was probably some talk then about her assisting in the editorial work of the *Review*, but it was not until the following spring that any definite understanding was arrived at'. In January 1851 Marian went to board at the Chapman's and remained there for three months.

From Chapman's diary it is amply evident that he believed that, during those months, she fell in love with him. Whether or no he exaggerated her feelings it is clear that their behaviour together aroused the jealousy both of his mistress Elisabeth and of the long-suffering wife, Susanna. Probably it was on this account that Marian left the household on 24 March 1851, on which day Chapman wrote in his diary:

M. departed today. I accompanied her to the railway. She was very sad, and hence made me feel so. She pressed me for some intimation of the state of my feelings. I told her that I felt great affection for her, but that I loved E and S also, though each in a different way. At this avowal she burst into tears. I tried to comfort her and reminded her of the dear friends she was returning to, but the train whirled her away very very sad.

Intolerable though Chapman is in his diary, and prone, to the point of mania, to imagine women in love with him, it yet seems probable that there was flame to account for the smoke. Marian Evans was thirty-one years old; she was quickly responsive to expressed affection; she needed to love and to be loved; and, both because she was a normal woman and because she was a woman of keen intelligence, she preferred the companionship of men. Chapman was an expert in taking advantage of all this. As to her tears (and Chapman refers more than once to outbursts of weeping) it is clear that she was emotionally excitable in a high degree, especially during these years between her father's death and her connection with Lewes. This fact can be discerned even in the pages of Cross; for instance, in a letter to the Brays in June 1852 she writes:

The opera, Chiswick Flower Show, the French play, and the Lyceum, all in one week, brought their natural consequences of head-ache and hysterics—all yesterday. At five o'clock I felt quite sure that life was unendurable. This morning, however, the weather and I are both better, having cried ourselves out and used up all our clouds; and I can even contemplate living six months longer.

Emotional excitability, fits of acute depression, headaches and hysterical tears were a price she paid until quite late in life for her exceptional gifts. At this time she endured the artist's heightened sensibility without the artist's creative outlet. It is likely also that her age and even her physical appearance led her to assume that she would never marry. Evidence both in portraits and in descriptions suggests that, though she was not ugly, she was the type of woman who looks ugly to herself in the glass. On the matter of her looks Mrs Lynn Linton is a good witness; at any rate she is one who is unlikely to err on the side of overpraise. In her letter to Herbert Spencer she writes:

It was only after her union with Mr Lewes that her beauty (in my eyes) came to the front. I remember telling Mr Linton once, after I had met and talked with her and Mr Lewes in St John's Wood, how infinitely ennobled she had become.

And in the *Temple Bar* [1] article, referring to George Eliot in her later life:

Plain in feature and singularly artificial in bearing she was loved by all men and passionately regarded by many. She might have changed her partner when she would, during Mr Lewes's life-time; and, after his death, if she had not married Mr Cross, she might have married others.

When Marian Evans looked in the glass, however, she would have seen none of this magnetic charm; only the plain features, that countenance which Locker-Lampson, somewhat redundantly tells us: 'was equine—she was rather like a horse; and her head had been intended for a much larger body—she was not a tall woman. . . . To my mind George Eliot was a plain woman.' [2]—Yet a young man who saw her as late as 1870 wrote:

The plainness vanished as soon as she smiled, and the tone of her voice was singularly sympathetic and harmonious.

However attractive Marian Evans may have been when her face was irradiated by sympathy and intelligence she saw a plain face in her mirror and suffered because she thought herself ugly. This would make her the more susceptible to Chapman's attentions.

---

[1] *Temple Bar*, 1885.
[2] *My Confidences*, Frederick Locker-Lampson, p. 312.

We shall not know how much nor for how long she cared for him, but it is likely that her return to Coventry was the result of some emotional relation between them. The facts that Chapman was at Coventry two months later, discussing the prospectus for the new *Westminster Review* with her, and that on 21 September she returned to his house where she remained for two years without, it appears, any further friction between her and Susanna or Elisabeth, suggests that the whole affair was ephemeral and superficial. Such as it was, or seems to have been, it modifies the too ponderous and pedagogic figure that emerges from the pages of Cross.

Probably the friendship with Herbert Spencer, which began almost immediately after her return to London, was helpful in relieving whatever tension there may have been. Beatrice Webb, in *My Apprenticeship*, quotes from her own diary of January 1885:

Herbert Spencer deliciously conscious about the 'Miss Evans' episode—asked me what was my impression of their relationship on reading those passages referring to him. Had wished John Cross to insert contradiction that there had ever been aught between them;

and, in a footnote, she adds:

It was an open secret that it was George Eliot who was in love with the philosopher, and when, on her death, newspaper paragraphs appeared implying that he had been one of her suitors he consulted my father about publishing the truth and nothing but the truth. 'My dear Spencer, you will be eternally damned if you do it,' replied my father.

In so far as one can ever know or state 'the truth' about human relationships it is possible to discern the truth about this one. Spencer was a high-minded and, in a sense, a simple-minded man and one does not feel the same need to discount his statements as one does with Chapman. In his *Autobiography* Spencer nowhere says that George Eliot was in love with him, but from all the evidence one can deduce that he could have won her if he had decided to do so. It also seems clear that, if he had been capable of falling in love at all, he would have done so with George Eliot. The fact that he was not capable of falling in love emerges clearly in his *Autobiography* and is confirmed by Beatrice Webb's character sketch in *My Apprenticeship*:

Poor Herbert Spencer. On reading the proof of his *Autobiography* I often think of that life given up to feeling his pulse and analysing his sensations, with no near friends to be all in all to him.... Strange that he should never have felt the sacrifice he was making.... 'I was never in love', he answered when I put the question straight: 'Were you never conscious of the wholesale sacrifice you were making, did you never long for those other forms of thought, feeling, action you were shut out from?' Strange—a nature with so perfect an intellect and little else—save friendliness and the uprightness of truth-loving mind. He has sometimes told me sadly that he has wondered at the weakness of his feelings, even of friendship and towards old friends and relations....

When Marian Evans began to see a good deal of Spencer, in 1851, the philosopher was thirty-one years old. The question of marriage, as an abstract speculation, was a good deal in his mind at this time. He tells us how, characteristically, he made lists of the advantages and disadvantages of the marriage state, in parallel columns. He decided that there were more reasons in favour of celibacy, and he wrote to his father:

On the whole I am quite decided not to be a drudge; and as I see no probability of being able to marry without being a drudge, why I have pretty well given up the idea.

It appears also that the question of his marriage was canvassed among his friends. He tells us that Chapman and Miss Evans arranged an introduction between him and a woman they thought eligible—the actors in this little comedy disliked each other on sight. On the other hand, he and Miss Evans liked each other mutually. Spencer's seriousness, integrity and even his coldness may have been especially welcome after the attentions of Chapman. (Compare Gwendolen Harleth's feelings in *Daniel Deronda* when Grandcourt proposes to her.) In any case friendship ripened quickly and afforded happiness to both parties in it: Spencer writes of her to his friend Lott in April 1852:

> Miss Evans whom you have heard me mention as the translatress of Strauss and as the most admirable woman, mentally, I ever met. We have been for some time past on very intimate terms. I am very frequently at Chapman's and the greatness of her intellect conjoined with her womanly qualities and manner generally keep me by her side most of the evening.

He goes on to give some account of their intimacy, telling us that:

> For some time before the date of this letter, the occasions of meeting had been multiplied by the opportunities I had for taking her to places of amusement. My free admissions for two, to the theatres and to the Royal Italian Opera, were, during these early months of 1852, much more used than they would otherwise have been, because I had frequently—indeed nearly always—the pleasure of her companionship in addition to the pleasure afforded by the performance.

It would be surprising if Marian Evans, with her warmly affectionate nature and her special emotional hunger at this time, did not respond with more warmth of feeling than he was capable of reciprocating. But Spencer was as upright as he was prim and Professor Gordon S. Haight quotes from a letter of hers written to the Brays, on Tuesday, 27 April 1852:

> We have agreed that we are not in love with each other, and that there is no reason why we should not have as much of each other's society as we like.

Cross, quoting from what must be the same letter, since it is also to the Brays and the last clause is identical, gives the date as 22 April, omits 'We have agreed that we are not in love with each other', and adds: 'he is a good, delightful creature and I always feel the better for being with him'.

We are left then with a clear impression of warm friendship between Miss Evans and Spencer, a friendship which afforded them mutual happiness and at some stage of which the question arose between them whether it was to lead to anything more.

Spencer came to an honest decision that he did not intend marriage: Miss Evans, wherever her feelings may have been tending, had them sufficiently within her control to accept that situation. All that Spencer tells us about her character and appearance helps to form a picture of what she was like at the time when she and G. H. Lewes first met. As regards her appearance his account confirms the opinion prevalent in other contemporary records that, though plain in feature, she often gave the impression of being beautiful:

> Striking by its power when in repose, her face was remarkably transfigured by a smile.[1]

The traits of character on which he lays stress are her self-control 'leading to an evenness of temper', her sympathy and her self-mistrust:

> Probably it was this last trait which prevented her from displaying her powers and her knowledge. The discovery of these had to be made gradually and incidentally.

In his view it was diffidence of her own powers which delayed her discovery of her vocation as a novelist; apparently he anticipated Lewes in perceiving that she had the gifts for this art:

> It was, I presume, her lack of self-confidence which led her, in those days, to resist my suggestion that she should write novels. I thought I saw in her many, if not all, of the needful qualifications in high degrees—quick observation, great powers of analysis, unusual and rapid intuition into others' states of mind, deep and broad sympathies, wit and humour, and wide culture. But she would not listen to any advice. She did not believe she had the required powers.

She was at this time devoting her intellectual energies to helping with the editing of *The Westminster Review* and to writing long and thoughtful articles and reviews for it. (Her articles for *The Westminster Review* are a great deal more solid and well written than her later work of this kind—such as the disappointing essays called *Impressions of Theophrastus Such*, published in 1879.) Her

[1] *Autobiography*, p. 395.

work in these years called upon and illustrated her reflective, not her creative powers, and Herbert Spencer tells us that he had 'known but few men with whom I could discuss a question in philosophy with more satisfaction'.

One of the few with whom he discussed such questions with at least equal satisfaction was George Henry Lewes. Friendship between the two men began in 1850, following upon Lewes's appreciative review of Spencer's *Social Statics* in *The Leader*. They found that they had many opinions and tastes in common and used to go for country excursions together, discussing philosophy. Spencer gives an impression of Lewes's social gifts which can be widely supported from other contemporary sources:

As a companion Lewes was extremely attractive. Interested in, and well informed upon, a variety of subjects; full of various anecdote; and an admirable mimic; it was impossible to be dull in his company.

No one ever accused Lewes of dullness; but some were alienated by his vivacity, his freedom of thought and behaviour, his lack of decorum and perhaps also by his extraordinary width of interests which made it easy to assume that this Jack-of-all-trades could be master of none.

The incalculable influence of George Henry Lewes on George Eliot makes it worth while to attempt to know him, even if he were not in his own right so well worth knowing. Time and chance have operated against an adequate appreciation of his unusual intellectual gifts. His union with George Eliot has itself been a factor in reducing his stature; he is remembered as a mere consort. The creative gift in her, which he did so much to discover and to foster, produced books of a timeless value, while his own voluminous works were in their nature ephemeral. It is true that he also attempted creative writing and has left two not quite unreadable novels (a third was uncompleted) and one blank verse tragedy which is a 'period piece'. But these offspring of his exuberant energy were products of fashion and of the need to earn a living; he had no creative genius and only average talent. His gift as an actor seems to have been on a par with his gift as novelist or dramatist; he had verve, imagination and, probably, an inherited histrionic temperament (his grandfather was a comedian). The talent was enough to make him an excellent mimic and an attractive *raconteur*; but not enough to make him an actor. He performed in Dickens's amateur companies and he appeared professionally in the part of Shylock at Manchester in 1849, with Barry Sullivan as Bassanio; in the same week in which he delivered a lecture in that city on the History of Philosophy. Francis Espinasse[1] tells us that his performance was ineffective, but that:

> There was originality in Lewes's conception of Shylock whom he endeavoured to represent as the champion and avenger of a persecuted race.

It seems unlikely that Lewes was the first to interpret Shylock in this way on the stage; but it is characteristic of him that he should have emphasized this aspect of the character (under his influence George Eliot's attitude to the Jews changed from antipathy to that over-romantic sympathy which produced *Daniel Deronda*). It is equally characteristic that he had the good sense to abandon the stage, either as dramatist or as performer, at the age of thirty-two and after one professional engagement. But though he failed as a performer he learnt enough about the stage to be an admirable critic of the drama. For four years (1850–4) he was a professional dramatic critic and two volumes[2] bear witness to the high level of his attainment in this field. Through their pages we can discern the quality of bygone actors: the unstable genius of Edmund Kean, Charles Kean's painstaking misapplication of a melodramatic talent to the high tragedy that lay beyond his reach, Rachel's overwhelming power, Macready's intelligent understanding of his parts, his physical advantages and the absence in him of that indefinable quality that transforms the good into the great actor. Lewes's own experience taught him that a good actor (like Ben Jonson's poet) is 'made as well as born': and that, as he says, 'people generally overrate a fine actor's

---

[1] *Literary Recollections and Sketches*, p. 284.
[2] *On Actors and the Art of Acting*, published in 1875; and *Dramatic Essays* by John Foster and G. H. Lewes, edited by William Archer and Robert Lowe.

genius and underrate his trained skill'. He knew that the actor's business is to enhance and perfect speech and gesture, not to imitate them:

> His art is one of representation, not of illusion... just as the language is poetry or choice prose, purified from hesitances, incoherences and imperfections of careless daily speech, so must his utterance be measured, musical and incisive—his manner typical and pictorial.

Clearly slovenly speech and casual gesture were already the vices of actors who thought it their business to imitate nature. Other all too familiar vices of performers are reproved by him, the murder of verse for instance:

> Her elocution is vicious. She chaunts instead of speaking, and her chaunt is unmusical. Instead of taking the rhythm from the sense, she puts one monotonous rhythm upon the verse, and lets the accent obey the impulses of the chaunt as if the voice mastered her instead of her mastering the voice;

or the declamation of Hamlet's too well known soliloquies. 'To be or not to be', Lewes asserts,

> ... is not a set speech to be declaimed to the pit, boxes and gallery, nor is it a moral thesis debated by Hamlet in intellectual freedom; yet one or other of these two mistakes is committed by all actors.... I think Shakespeare's genius was too eminently dramatic to have substituted an oration for an exhibition of Hamlet's state of mind. The speech is passionate, not reflective, and it should be spoken as if the thoughts were wrung from the agonies of a soul hankering after suicide as an escape from evils, yet terrified at the dim sense of greater evils after death.

Lewes knew enough about acting to be a constructive critic of the craft and he knew enough about drama to stand aloof from contemporary fashion. In the fifties, when he was writing his dramatic reviews for *The Leader*, the poetic drama of the Jacobean Age and Victor Hugo's romantic melodramas were all the rage; every poetaster was ready to attempt blank verse tragedy (as

Lewes himself had done in *The Noble Heart*). Lewes is boldly heretical; he declares his conviction that:

The greatest injury yet sustained by the English drama was the revival of admiration for the old English dramatists.... Whoever has more than a second-hand acquaintance with Kyd, Peele, Marlowe, Webster, Dekker, Ford, Marston, Chapman, Heywood, Middleton, Shirley, Cyril Tourneur and the rest, will probably agree with us that their plays are as poor in construction (artistic as well as theatric) as they are resplendent in imagery and weighty lines—that their characters are *sketched* rather than *developed*—that their situations are for the most part violent, horrible, and clumsily prepared, and that besides being wearisome in reading, they are essentially unfit for the modern stage.

But while Lewes had, as William Archer says, 'a passion for the theatre at once enlightened and enlightening', dramatic criticism at no time absorbed the whole of his energies. Before 1850 he had already published his first edition of the *Biographical History of Philosophy* which was enlarged and republished at intervals throughout his life, and he was engaged on his other *magnum opus*, *The Life of Goethe*.

Lewes's *Biographical History of Philosophy* first appeared in 1845–6 in four volumes of *Knight's Weekly Volume Series*. In it he sketches the history of philosophy, with biographical notes on the philosophers, from the earliest times to the advent of Auguste Comte. His book is Comtist in intention, accepting Comte's view of the progress of human thought through three successive stages; first the religious or *magical* explanation of phenomena, next the metaphysical stage in which man reasons about abstract principles and endeavours to define the nature of God, and third positivist in which no truth is sought for beyond what can be deduced from experience and applied to further the well-being of mankind. Sir Leslie Stephen, in the *Dictionary of National Biography*, notes that Lewes's book contains 'rather the impressions of a very quick and brilliant journalist than the investigations of a profound student', but adds that 'the vivacity of the writing and the skill with which the personal history of philosophers was connected with the history of their speculations gave a deserved popularity to the book'. Lewes's twentieth-century biographer, Miss Anna Theresa Kitchel, found that his *Biographical History* still retained its popularity in the nineteen-thirties; when she asked for a copy in the Charing Cross Road she was told:

'We can't keep them in stock, madam. The London University students buy them up. You see, madam, they can *understand* Lewes.'

In his endeavour to popularize knowledge Lewes was, for once, swimming with the stream. In the mid-nineteenth century dissemination of knowledge was as commendable as thrift. Nor was his range of inquiry as unusual then as now, but the book has some characteristics which are all his own. To begin with it is readable, not merely because it is an intelligible short-cut to a difficult subject, but because the easy, intimate style conveys the writer's personality and communicates his own enthusiasm. It is also refreshingly honest. When some school of philosophy has proved too drasty even for Lewes's voracious appetite, he readily admits that he speaks of it only at second-hand; nor is there ever any pretence that he is writing a history without *parti pris*. Such a book was bound to be superseded, but it made a serious contribution to the spread of knowledge in its own time; in this book and in other of his works Lewes was one of the first to familiarize English readers not only with Comte but also with Spinoza.

Francis Espinasse gives in his *Literary Recollections* an account of Lewes's first acquaintance with Spinoza's work which is of especial interest because we find the story, only very slightly transmuted, in *Daniel Deronda*. Espinasse derives it in the main from Lewes's own account in *The Fortnightly Review*, where Lewes wrote in 1866:

About thirty years ago a small club of students held weekly meetings in the parlour of a tavern in Red Lion Square, Holborn, where the varied questions of philosophy were discussed with earnestness, if not with insight. The club was extremely simple in its rules and informal in its proceedings. Its members were men whose sole point of junction was the Saturday meeting, and whose sole object was the amicable collision of contending views on subjects which at one time or other perplex and stimulate all reflecting minds. On every other day in the week their paths were widely divergent. One kept a second-hand bookstall, rich in free-thinking literature; another was a journeyman watch-maker; a third lived on a moderate income; a fourth was a bootmaker; a fifth 'penned a stanza when he should engross'; a sixth[1] studied anatomy and many other things, with vast aspirations and no very definite career before him. Although thus widely separated, those divergent paths converged every Saturday towards the little parlour in Red Lion Square, and the chimes of midnight were drowned in the pleasant noises of argument and laughter; argument sometimes loud and angry, but on these occasions always terminating in laughter, which cleared the air with its explosions. Seated round the fire smoking their cigars and pipes, and drinking coffee, grog, or ale, without chairman or president, without fixed form of debate, and with a general tendency to talk all at once when the discussion grew animated, these philosophers did really strike out sparks which illuminated each other's minds; they permitted no displays of rhetoric such as generally make debating societies intolerable; they came for philosophic talk, and they talked.

Among these intellectual explorers one is mentioned who was later to suggest to George Eliot the character of Mordecai. He was a German Jew called Cohn

... whom [Lewes wrote] we all admired as a man of astonishing subtlety and logical force no less than of great personal worth. He remains in my memory as a type of philosophic dignity. A calm, meditative, amiable man, by trade a journeyman watchmaker, very poor, with weak eyes and chest; grave and gentle in demeanour; incorruptible, even by the seductions of vanity. I habitually think of him in con-nection with Spinoza, almost as much on account of his personal characteristics as because to him I owe my first acquaintance with the Hebrew thinker. My admiration for him was of that enthusiastic temper which in youth we feel for our intellectual leaders. I loved his weak eyes and low voice; I venerated his great calm intellect. He was the

[1] Espinasse adds 'doubtless Lewes himself'.

only man I did not contradict in the impatience of argument. An immense pity and fervid indignation filled me as I came away from his attic in one of the Holborn Courts, where I had seen him in the pinching poverty of his home, with his German wife and two little black-eyed children: indignantly I railed against society, which could allow so great an intellect to withdraw itself from nobler work and waste the precious hours in mending watches. But he was wiser in his resignation than I was in my young indignation. Life was hard to him as to all of us; but he was content to earn a miserable living by handicraft and keep his soul serene. I learned to understand him better when I learned the story of Spinoza's life.

Cohn found a German work expounding the philosophy of Spinoza on a London bookstall. He transmitted the doctrines to the Club.

It was the more interesting to me [Lewes continues] because I happened to be hungering for some knowledge of this theological pariah, partly, no doubt, because he was an outcast, for as I was then suffering the social persecution which embitters all departure from accepted creeds, I had a rebellious sympathy with all outcasts, and partly because I had casually met with a passage, quoted for reprobation, in which Spinoza maintained the subjective nature of evil, a passage which, to my mind, lighted up that perplexed question.

Espinasse adds that:

At last Lewes lighted, in an old bookshop, on a small crown quarto, *Spinoza opera posthuma*, and mastered at first-hand the system the rudiments of which he had learned from Cohn. In 1843 (aetat. 29) Lewes made Spinoza the subject of an article which was the earliest modern attempt in England to rehabilitate that profound and original thinker, whose system even David Hume spoke of as 'infamous'. Soon after this acquaintance with Spinoza, and doubtless to study German philosophy in the land of its birth, he went to Germany, acquiring a perfect knowledge of its language. His early residence in Brittany had made him a master of French.

Professor W. R. Sorley[1] tells us that in the mid-nineteenth century 'Leibniz and even Spinoza were hardly more than

[1] *The Cambridge History of English Literature*, vol. XIV, p. 8.

names' in England. 'Since the time of Descartes, continental thought had had little effect upon English philosophy.' But in the intellectual sphere in which Marian Evans had lived since she went to Coventry, and which was contiguous with that in which Lewes moved, this provincialism of thought was breaking down. Before she met Lewes she was, as has been noted, already an admirer of Spinoza and had begun to translate some of his works. Both she and G. H. Lewes recognized in Spinoza a forerunner of all that is most humane in Utilitarian philosophy; they welcomed his insistence in the *Ethics* on the unreality (or relativity) of evil:

> With regard to Good and Evil, these terms indicate nothing positive in things considered in themselves, nor are they anything else than modes of thought, or notions which we form from the comparison of one thing with another. For one and the same thing may at the same time be both good and evil or indifferent. Music, for example, is good to a melancholy person, bad to one in mourning, while to a deaf man it is neither good nor bad. But although things are not so, we must retain these words. For since we desire to form for ourselves an idea of man upon which we may look as a model of human nature, it will be of some service to us to retain these expressions. . . .By *good*, therefore, I understand in the following pages everything which we are certain is a means by which we may approach nearer and nearer to the model of human nature we set before us. By *evil*, on the contrary, I understand everything which we are certain hinders us from reaching that model.[1]

Equally congenial to them both was Spinoza's insistence that:

> It is the part of a wise man, I say, to refresh and invigorate himself with moderate and pleasant eating and drinking, with sweet scents and the beauty of green plants, with ornament, with music, with sports, with the theatre and with all things of this kind which one man may enjoy without hurting another.[2]

Besides introducing Spinoza to English readers Lewes was also the first to make the Philosophy of Comte widely known. Herbert Spencer had read none of Comte's writings in 1850 when he was writing *Social Statics*; the first attempt to translate

---

[1] Spinoza, *Ethics*, Pt. IV.   [2] Ibid.

Comte's work into English was Harriet Martineau's translation and condensation, *The Positive Philosophy*, in 1853, and Lewes himself brought out his summary, *Comte's Philosophy of the Sciences*, in the same year; but he had already made Comte known and done useful propaganda for him in his *Biographical History of Philosophy*. To the modern reader the intellectual stature of Comte is dwarfish when seen beside Spinoza, but they both appealed to Lewes because they both make speculation the servant of ethics. The nineteenth-century philosopher has not worn so well as his seventeenth-century predecessor, perhaps because Spinoza, despite the forbidding Euclidean form of his work, is a poet and a mystic; the foundations of his thought rest upon imagination and wisdom rather than intellect and knowledge. But to Lewes, as to other of his contemporaries, Comte's comprehensive knowledge and extraordinary powers of systematizing it seemed to extend and illuminate the whole field of human inquiry.

Lewes's interest in Goethe presumably took serious hold of his mind when he went to Germany in 1843. He worked on the life for ten years and it was completed and published soon after his union with Marian Evans. The *Life of Goethe* has, like Lewes's other books, been inevitably superseded as new information has accumulated; but when Sir Leslie Stephen wrote his article on Lewes for the *D.N.B.* it was still 'the standard work in English upon the subject'. It succeeds in painting a convincing portrait of a man of genius and of forceful idiosyncratic character, and Lewes's criticisms of Goethe's works are genuine expressions of his own experience and therefore (whether just or unjust) retain their vitality. He is never overawed by his subject nor by his contemporary critics, but is content to give a clear and reasoned account of his own opinions. For instance, he is in the main unimpressed, or at least unconvinced, by the second part of *Faust*; the first part, in which the whole meaning is implicit in character and situation, moved him profoundly; the more nebulous second part, from which his contemporary critics were eliciting a bewildering number of 'meanings' (a practice which had begun

in Goethe's lifetime and about which the poet had kept an
oracular silence) left Lewes sceptical. He recognized that Goethe's
own comment about uncomprehending readers might be
relevant:

The most legible writing being illegible in the twilight;

but he nevertheless declared his own judgement that Goethe had
not, in Part II, mastered his subject. As Francis Espinasse writes:

Whether he was dealing with literature, philosophy, or science,
Lewes was never an echo of his predecessors or contemporaries.

And this it is that keeps so much of his work still readable.

When Marian Evans first met Lewes in 1851 he already had the
reputation of a gifted and versatile man of letters. His articles on
a wide range of subjects appeared in *The Edinburgh Review*, *The
Westminster Review* and *The Fortnightly Review* and in 1849–50
he and Thornton Hunt were largely responsible for *The Leader*.
The wide spread of his interests militated against his being taken
seriously by the learned even in the mid-nineteenth century, when
specialization was less of an occupational disease than now. A
would-be novelist, dramatist, actor, and dramatic critic who had
also studied medicine and written a history of philosophy was
inevitably suspected of superficiality. The fact that he could also
write or talk about the literature of Greece, Rome, France, Germany, Italy and Spain (he had a good reading knowledge of all
these languages) only added to the suspicion that he knew nothing
thoroughly. Yet Herbert Spencer found him worth attention on
the subjects he himself best understood. The Carlyles on the
other hand, who knew Lewes well, thought him a figure of fun,
though entertaining and likeable:

he is the most amusing little fellow in the whole world—if you only
look over his unparalleled *impudence* which is not impudence at all but
man of genius *bonhomie*....He is the best mimic in the world and full
of famous stories, and no spleen or envy, or *bad* thing in him, so see
that you receive him with open arms in spite of his immense ugliness.

Jane Carlyle wrote this in 1849; but after the publication of *The Life of Goethe*, Espinasse tells us, Lewes's reputation was much enhanced. Carlyle appreciated its 'undeniable merits none the less because it was dedicated to him'. Lewes, however, did not foster his reputation by doing more work in the same field as a biographer, a literary critic or an interpreter of German romanticism; he characteristically turned to quite other pursuits and became absorbed in studying marine biology. His researches were sufficiently fruitful for Darwin to quote him with approval in *The Origin of Species*. In the latter part of his life Lewes's intellectual energy was mainly devoted to scientific work embodied in the five volumes of his *Problems of Life and Mind*.

Contemporary records give a vivid impression of what Lewes was like socially in the years preceding his union with Marian Evans. The impact he made on his contemporaries is not unlike the impact Ladislaw made on the inhabitants of *Middlemarch*. His cosmopolitan tastes and unconventional manners were entertaining; to many they were also shocking. Eliza Lynn Linton when at the age of eighteen, a crude provincial girl, she first met the Leweses, was definitely shocked, nor did she ever quite get over her sense that Lewes was outrageous:

He was the first of the audacious men of my acquaintance, and about the most extreme. He had neither shame nor reticence in his choice of subjects, but would discourse on the most delicate matters of physiology with no more perception that he was transgressing the bounds of propriety than if he had been a learned savage. I heard more startling things from Lewes, in full conclave of young and old, married and single, men and women, than I had ever dreamed of or heard hinted at before. And I know that men complained of his after-dinner talk and anecdotes as being beyond the licence accorded to, or taken by, even the boldest talkers of the mess-table and the club smoking-room. He did not go so far as this in public, but he went very far; and to a young girl, fresh from a country life where the faint echoes of 'plums, prunes and prisms' still lingered, it was all embarrassing and 'shocking' enough.[1]

[1] Mrs Lynn Linton, *My Literary Life in London*, p. 18.

The Carlyles were more experienced and less easily shocked, but Lewes's freedom of manners is evident in Jane Carlyle's descriptions of him: 'an airy loose-tongued merry-hearted being, with more sail than ballast'.[1] Frederick Locker-Lampson at a later date found Lewes's dress and manners offensive and was only reluctantly amused by him:

I did not find him agreeable; but he once made Tennyson and me laugh heartily by his description of a certain 'noble lord'. . . . Lewes had been an actor, and he imitated the voice and gesture.[2]

He did not correspond to Locker-Lampson's conception of an English gentleman:

He had long hair, and his dress was an unlovely compromise between morning and evening costume, combining the less pleasing points of both.

Even those who subsequently grew to like and to respect Lewes often began, as George Eliot did herself, by thinking him light-minded and flippant. 'The expression of his contempt for cant,' Espinasse writes, 'had he been cynical, would have been bitter, but in his case it took the form of levity, and thus exposed him, with serious people, to the charge of flippancy. After meeting him for the first time, Margaret Fuller described him as "a witty French flippant sort of man". It was not until she had known him for more than a year that George Eliot herself wrote of Lewes "he has quite won my regard".[3]

In the light of all that is now known both of George Eliot and of Lewes it is not surprising that they should have loved each other, nor that their union should have been the main source of happiness for both during the twenty-six years that remained of Lewes's life. But whenever Lewes has been thought of as merely volatile and flippant, George Eliot as merely an austere, melancholy moralist, it has seemed hard to explain a union between them which involved a defiance of law and convention and the risk of social ostracism. As a matter of fact such a risk would

---

[1] *Letters of Jane Welsh Carlyle*, 25 April 1850.
[2] *My Confidences*, Frederick Locker-Lampson, p. 313.
[3] *Literary Recollections*, Francis Espinasse, p. 277.

have been more likely to strengthen Marian Evans's resolution (as it would have done Maggie's or Dorothea's) once she was sure of their mutual love and convinced that their union would destroy no one else's happiness.

When Lewes and Marian Evans first met his marriage had been in ruins for two years; Jane Carlyle's quick perceptions had discerned the cooling of affection as early as 1849:

> I used to think these Leweses a perfect pair of love-birds always cuddling together on the same perch—to speak figuratively—but the female love-bird appears to have hopped off to some distance and to be now taking a somewhat critical view of her shaggy little mate.

Agnes Lewes, acting in accordance with the belief in free love that her husband at one time shared with her and perhaps taught her, had transferred her affection to his friend Thornton Hunt and had had a child by him. In accordance with their belief, Lewes had condoned the offence and neither now nor later, publicly nor in his private diary, did he show any sign of resentment; he was devoted to his own three sons and he accepted Thornton's as a part of the family; but unconventional views, though they may govern behaviour, do not alter human nature nor mitigate suffering. Lewes, writing of Herbert Spencer in his journal in 1859, says:

> I owe him a debt of gratitude. My acquaintance with him was the brightest ray in a very dreary, *wasted* period of my life. I had given up all ambition whatever, lived from hand to mouth and thought the evil of each day sufficient.

Lewes and Herbert Spencer spent long hours and days together and talked philosophy; but Spencer specifically states that he knew nothing at this time of Lewes's domestic life, adding:

> But alike then and afterwards I was impressed by his forgiving temper and generosity. Whatever else may be thought, it is undeniable that he discharged the responsibilities which devolved upon him with great conscientiousness, and at much cost in self-sacrifice, notwithstanding circumstances which many men would have made a plea for repudiating them.

Eliza Lynn Linton is a more telling witness to Lewes's loyal and generous behaviour to his first wife, since she so obviously disliked him. She pays her tribute to Lewes in the same paragraph (in her article in *Temple Bar* 1885) in which she begins by abusing him:

> Had Mr Lewes been a different man—had he one touch of delicacy of conscience, of sensitiveness of fibre—had he failed a hair's breadth in his resolute determination to get what he wanted, to make the best job of life possible, and to play his part like the finished actor he was—she [i.e. Marian Evans] would not have had the strength of character to take the step she did.

And one wonders what precisely Mrs Linton understood by 'delicacy of conscience' and 'sensitiveness of fibre' since she continues in the same paragraph:

> ...she had the devotion of a man whose love had in it that element of adoration and self-suppression which is dearest of all to a woman like George Eliot, at once jealous and dependent, demanding exclusive devotion and needing incessant care—but ready to give all she had in return. This power of self-suppression for the sake of a woman had been already shown in Mr Lewes's conduct to his wife—the true history of which will never now be written. Falling in love with Marian Evans, he grew tired of the singular part he had voluntarily played for some years, and so swept the board clear.

Lewes 'swept the board clear' in so far as he and Marian Evans determined to live together as man and wife in defiance of the law. Not only would divorce at this date have required an Act of Parliament and so entailed expense far beyond Lewes's means, but he had condoned Agnes's breach of faith for some considerable time (possibly two years) before he met Marian Evans. After their union his sons remained with Agnes until they were old enough to be sent to school, the two elder ones in 1856 and the youngest in 1857, by which time all three boys were at school in Switzerland and were spending their holidays with their father and Marian. From henceforward it is she rather than Agnes who stands in the relation of a mother to them. Agnes had a son and three daughters by Thornton Hunt and Lewes contributed to her and their maintenance for the rest of his life; after his death Marian continued to do so, and after her death, Charles Lewes, the eldest son of George and Agnes, paid the allowance until his death in 1891. Not only did Lewes continue to support his wife, but he remained in friendly and advisory relations with her and wrote his last letter to her two months before his death. Entries in Lewes's diary show that difficulties arose; Thornton Hunt appears to have inherited his father's lack of money-sense; in the diary, 5 December 1856, Lewes writes:

Have been agitated and distressed lately by finding Agnes £150 in debt, mainly owing to T's defalcations.

In 1858 she had exceeded an increased allowance by £184. But though the friendship between Hunt and Lewes gradually cooled and died, he continued to watch over Agnes's fortunes with solicitous kindness until his death.

Marian Evans was first introduced to Lewes at a bookshop in September 1851 and after that Herbert Spencer frequently brought him to Chapman's house. Friendship ripened steadily between them; at first it was Lewes's gaiety and charm that pleased Marian rather in spite of herself, since his behaviour seemed flippant. It is not until two years later, 28 March 1853, that the letters quoted by Cross express a strong regard for him:

People are very good to me. Mr Lewes especially is kind and attentive, and has quite won my regard, after having a good deal of my vituperation. Like a few other people in the world, he is much better than he seems. A man of heart and conscience wearing a mask of flippancy.

In the autumn of that year she moved from Chapman's house into lodgings, possibly in order to be more independent. She was helping Lewes to correct the proofs for *The Leader* and in November she told Chapman that she wished to sever her connection with *The Westminster Review*; he persuaded her to go on until April, in which month she found herself hard-driven, as Lewes was ill and she was trying to do his work as well as her own. Apparently by May she had decided, or almost decided, to go abroad with him; she writes to Charles Bray, 'It is quite possible that I may wish to go to the continent, or twenty other things'. In July 1854 Lewes and she set sail for Germany. Cross prints her brief farewell note to the Brays dated 20 July 1854:

Dear Friends,—all three—I have only time to say goodbye, and God bless you. *Poste Restante*, Weimar, for the next six weeks, and afterwards Berlin. Ever your loving and grateful Marian.

After that Cross prints from no other letter to the Brays until one to Mrs Bray dated 4 September 1855, fourteen months after Marian left England. The extract shows that the passage of time had not led the Brays to accept the situation or to understand why Marian had joined Lewes. Her letter is explanatory:

If there is any one relation of my life which is and always has been profoundly serious, it is my relation to Mr Lewes. It is, however, natural enough that you should mistake me in many ways, for not only are you unacquainted with Mr Lewes's real character and the course of his actions, but also it is several years now since you and I were much together, and it is possible that the modifications my mind has undergone may be quite in the opposite direction of what you imagine. No one can be better aware than yourself that it is possible for two people to hold different opinions on momentous subjects with equal sincerity, and an equally earnest conviction that their respective opinions are alone the truly moral ones. If we differ on the subject of the marriage laws, I at least can believe of you that you cleave to what you believe to be good; and I don't know of anything in the nature of your views that should prevent you from believing the same of me. *How far* we differ, I think we neither of us know, for I am ignorant of your precise views; and apparently you attribute to me both feelings and opinions which are not mine. We cannot set each other quite right in this matter in letters, but one thing I can tell you in few words. Light and easily broken ties are what I neither desire theoretically nor could live for practically. Women who are satisfied with such ties do *not* act as I have done. That any unworldly, unsuperstitious person who is sufficiently acquainted with the realities of life can pronounce my relation to Mr Lewes immoral, I can only understand by remembering how subtle and complex are the influences that mould opinion. But I *do* remember this: and I indulge in no arrogant or uncharitable thoughts about those who condemn us, even though we might have expected a somewhat different verdict. From the majority of persons, of course, we never looked for anything but condemnation. We are leading no life of self-indulgence, except indeed that, being happy in each other, we find everything easy. We are working hard to provide for others better than we provide for ourselves, and to fulfil every responsibility that lies upon us. Levity and pride would not be a sufficient basis for that. Pardon me if, in vindicating myself from some unjust conclusions, I seem too cold and self-asserting. I should not care to vindicate myself if I did not love you and desire to relieve you of the pain which you say these conclusions have given you. Whatever I may have misinterpreted before, I do not misinterpret your letter this morning, but read in it nothing else than love and kindness towards me, to which my heart fully answers, yes....

From this extract it is easy to see what were the degree and nature of the opposition from the Brays which had continued throughout the year. That it should have been so is the more surprising in the light of a letter (printed for the first time by Professor Haight in *George Eliot and John Chapman*) which she wrote eleven months before to Charles Bray, dated 23 October 1854, from Weimar. The letter opens with a request for advice about her banking account and continues:

It is possible that you have already heard a report prevalent in London that Mr Lewes has 'run away' from his wife and family. I wish you to be in possession of the facts which will enable you to contradict this report whenever it reaches you. Since we left England he has been in constant correspondence with his wife; she has had all the money due to him in London; and his children are his principal thought and anxiety. Circumstances with which I am not concerned, and which have arisen since he left England, have led him to determine on a separation from Mrs Lewes, but he has never contemplated that separation as a total release from responsibility towards her.[1] On the contrary he has been anxiously awaiting restoration to health that he may once more work hard, not only to provide for his children, but

---

[1] I can suggest no explanation of this sentence. The known facts would suggest that the separation was decided on before Lewes left England and that the 'circumstances' of Mrs Lewes's cohabitation with Thornton Hunt for the two previous years were sufficient to account for it.

to supply his wife's wants so far as that is not done by another. I have seen all the correspondence between them, and it has assured me that his conduct as a husband has not been only irreproachable, but generous and self-sacrificing to a degree far beyond any standard fixed by the world. This is the simple truth and no flattering picture drawn by my partiality.

I have been long enough with Mr Lewes to judge of his character on adequate grounds, and there is therefore no absurdity in offering my opinion as evidence that he is worthy of high respect. He has written to Carlyle and Robert Chambers stating as much of the truth as he can without severely inculpating other persons concerned; Arthur Helps, who has been here since we came, already knew the whole truth, and I trust that these three rational friends will be able in time to free his character from the false imputations which malice and gossip have cast upon it.

Of course many silly myths are already afloat about me, in addition to the truth, which of itself would be thought matter for scandal. I am quite unconcerned about them except as they may cause pain to my real friends. If you can hear of anything that I have said, done, or written in relation to Mr Lewes, beyond the simple fact that I am attached to him and that I am living with him, do me the justice to believe that it is false. Mr and Mrs Chapman are the only persons to whom I have ever spoken of his private position and of my relation to him, and the only influence I should ever dream of exerting over him as to his conduct towards his wife and children is that of stimulating his conscientious care for them if it needed any stimulus.

Pray pardon this long letter on a painful subject. I felt it a duty to write it.

I am ignorant how far Cara and Sara may be acquainted with the state of things, and how they may feel towards me. I am quite prepared to accept the consequences of a step which I have deliberately taken and to accept them without irritation or bitterness. The most painful consequences will, I know, be the loss of friends. If I do not write, therefore, understand that it is because I do not desire to obtrude myself.

Write to me soon and let me know how things are with you. I am full of affection towards you all, and whatever you may think of me I shall always be

Your true and grateful friend,
Marian Evans.

The subsequent history of the friendship with the Brays will be clearer when Professor Haight publishes the complete edition of George Eliot's letters, which he promises in his Preface. Cross prints an extract from a friendly, chatty letter to Mrs Bray, 5 April 1857; and two from letters to Charles about rumours that she is the author of the *Scenes* and of *Adam Bede*, rumours which she believes he has been instrumental in propagating. This is in March 1858; Charles Bray sends a prompt denial and she thanks him, adding: 'If I withhold anything from my friends which it would gratify them to know, you will believe, I hope, that I have good reasons for doing so....' It is clear that the friendship between her and the Brays was renewed, though not whether it was ever as warm as hitherto. Marian had expected her rationalist friends to have more confidence in her moral judgement than they actually showed and she had assumed that they shared (consistently with their general outlook) her own criterion which assured her that her breach of the law and of the social conventions was justified because it increased the happiness of most of the people concerned and damaged the happiness of none of them. What actually happened over the course of years is best summed up by Mrs Lynn Linton who was herself cold-shouldered by society for no worse a fault than living apart from her husband:

Society was at first as stern to George Eliot after her domestic intimacy with Lewes as Mrs Carlyle had been. I remember hearing an instance of this some years after the connection was formed. Lewes and George Eliot once thought of establishing a domicile in Kent and a south-eastern, semi-suburb of London much tenanted by wealthy city people was chosen. When news of the intention of the distinguished pair reached the denizens of the region a council of male and female heads of families was held to consider whether George Eliot should be 'received'. It was decided that she should not. As is well known, public opinion altered in course of time, and, ultimately, the lady rejected by London citizens was courted and caressed by daughters of Queen Victoria herself.

Despite the social difficulties that ensued and the financial anxieties of the early years, the union with Lewes marked the achievement for Marian Evans of emotional equilibrium. Her release from dogmatic religious beliefs had already given her intellectual serenity and there were no subsequent intellectual influences that caused a reorientation of her beliefs comparable with what had culminated at Coventry. Metaphysical speculations did not disturb her henceforth, not because she believed she had solved the problems raised by them, but because she held such problems to be insoluble and was content to devote her own attention to

> the world
> Of all of us—the place where in the end
> We find our happiness or not at all.[1]

When, in 1859, Darwin's *Origin of Species* was published and caused so much disturbance and controversy, it was to her only a further confirmation of the development theory she had long ago accepted:

It makes an epoch, as the expression of his thorough adhesion, after long years of study, to the Doctrine of Development—and not the adhesion of an anonym like the author of the *Vestiges*, but of a long-celebrated naturalist.... It will have a great effect in the scientific world, causing a thorough and open discussion of a question about which people have hitherto felt timid. So the world gets on step by step towards brave clearness and honesty! But to me the Development theory, and all other explanations of processes by which things came to be, produce a feeble impression compared with the mystery that underlies the processes.[2]

The comment illustrates her 'meliorist' (to use her own word) belief in the gradual advance of the race towards clear thought and its consequences, as well as her 'agnosticism' about the mystery of creation. She was now ready to devote herself to the work for which she was best fitted, the embodiment of her own vision of human life in works of prose fiction. Her material was the human life she knew intimately, the experience of which had

[1] Wordsworth, *The Prelude*, bk. XI.
[2] Letter to Mrs Bodichon, 5 December 1859; Cross, vol. II, p. 148.

conditioned her own growth to maturity of thought and feeling. Whenever in her future career she chose a subject that led her to look away from English rural and provincial life she was liable to fail. Within that sphere her sense of humour, her compassion and her moral judgement were unerring; she fully understood the conditions and the types of character and action they gave rise to.

In 1856 she showed Lewes the beginning of *Amos Barton*. He was previously convinced that she had several of the gifts necessary for a writer of fiction but he doubted her dramatic power; the fragment she showed him gave sufficient evidence that she could write excellent dialogue. The success of the volume *Scenes of Clerical Life* comprising *Amos Barton*, *Mr Gilfil's Love Story* and *Janet's Repentance* was even beyond their hopes. She was immediately recognized both by the critics and by her fellow-artists as an important and original writer. She is probably the last English novelist to be equally esteemed by the contemporary critics and enjoyed by the general public and few can have leapt so immediately into fame with their first book.

Part II

The Novels

CHAPTER IV

VISION AND DESIGN

WHEN we read George Eliot's novels for the first time we are likely to be too much absorbed in the unfolding of the story to be conscious of any peculiar characteristics of her vision of life or her method of presenting it. Like most of the great Victorian novelists, she has the spell-binding power of the Ancient Mariner; we are forced to attend, the world in which her characters move becomes the real world, unquestioningly accepted. The principal characters take their place in the foreground, our sympathies are firmly engaged for them and we are carried forward by that curiosity which novel readers share with children, the desire to know what happens next. Only when the book is closed and we cease to participate in the life of Hayslope, St Ogg's or Middlemarch can we begin to inquire what makes up the characteristic impression of a George Eliot novel; by then the spell is broken. But it is well to remember that her books are great works of fiction, partly because they have this magic; no analysis can reproduce it any more than an analysis of a poem can reproduce the effect of poetry. With fiction as with poetry the first necessity (if the work is to become an effective part of our own experience) is to submit to the spell: intellectual appreciation and evaluation follow after. It is, of course, the story, not the mere plot, that works the spell. The plot is preconceived by the author and can be summarized by the critic, but the stories, George Eliot herself tells us, 'grow in me like plants'. It is the growth of the plant, the gradual unfolding of character in its environment, that compels attention, not the mere concatenation of events. The story-teller works her will on us because we are convinced that these people and this town or village exist. The novels, like any other stories that beguile us, provide us with the pleasure of disinterested sympathy. When we read of the

77

sufferings of fictitious, or, for that matter, of historical characters, we can indulge in the natural human tendency to sympathize without any possibility of being required to act. In so far as an unimaginative hardness of heart is normal, it is probably the result of unconscious self-protection against such a demand, and the satisfaction following upon reading a fiction or witnessing a drama suggests that, when there is no need to be on the defensive, we enjoy being made to understand our fellow-sufferers. The ultimate value of such aesthetic experience will depend upon how far the pleasurable exercise—playing at sympathy—can affect our conduct in the workaday world. The immediate effect of reading George Eliot's novels is, then, one which her works have in common with all successful fiction, it is hard to put the book down. Jane Carlyle read the *Scenes of Clerical Life* sitting up in bed with a high temperature and a sore throat, and wrote to the unknown author:

> You will believe that the book needed to be something more than a 'new novel' for me; that I *could* at my years, and after so much reading, read it in positive torment, and be beguiled by it of the torment.[1]

That power to beguile persisted and increased (with partial lapses in *Romola* and *Daniel Deronda*) and it is only when we shake ourselves free from the beguilement that we notice that the vision of life we have shared has its individual character. Despite all the differences between George Eliot's novels, certain broad resemblances mark them as the product of a single mind.

There is, first of all, a resemblance in the way she shapes her novels and consequently in the total impression any one of them leaves with the reader. When we try, after an interval, to recall any one of them we find ourselves thinking as much about the life of a village or a provincial town, or of the interrelation of groups of families, as about the central drama. George Eliot herself said, with reference to *Romola*: 'It is the habit of my imagination to strive after as full a vision of the medium in which a character moves as of the character itself', and that habit accounts for the depth and breadth of the vision of life she com-

[1] Cross, vol. II, p. 10.

municates. As a matter of fact the word 'strive', appropriate to
Romola where the 'medium' was fifteenth-century Florence
whose habits of life and thought she had to reconstruct on a basis
of research, is misleading when applied to her English novels. The
rural and provincial life of England she had known from childhood: her imagination contained it rather than strove after it.
But it is clear that she gave as much attention to presenting the
outer circle of her design as the inner. The outer circle within
which the dramatic situation is contained, is an organic human
society and her novels are deeply imbued with the spirit of a
particular place and time.

Adam Bede is the earliest and simplest example of the typical
George Eliot form. The life of Hayslope envelops the tragedy.
We come to know all grades of its society, artisans, labourers,
farmers, rector, schoolmaster, innkeeper and squire. It is an
active community in which most men or women have work to
do and their character is affected by that work. That character is
also the product of religious influences; we become aware of the
impact of Methodism upon the inhabitants of Hayslope and of
the more subtly pervasive influence of traditional Anglicanism.
In the Third Book the whole community is assembled at Donnithorne Chase to celebrate the young squire's coming of age; by
that time the pattern of living out of which the central characters
emerge is clearly established and their drama is already under way.
After the climax, when Hetty Sorrel has been condemned to
death, reprieved and deported and another author would feel
that the work was complete, there is a Sixth Book, balancing the
Third. In it the rhythm of Hayslope life is re-established and,
with the inevitable gaps made by the intervening event, a Harvest
supper reassembles the same community as celebrated the young
squire's birthday. The central tragedy is intimately connected
with this background. The full effect of Arthur Donnithorne's
yielding to the sensuous appeal of the pretty child-like Hetty
and of all that ensues depends upon the relation of both characters
to their world. The pride and well-grounded self-respect of the
Poysers, established in the reader's mind by the vivid pictures of

their surroundings, their working day, their home life, their Sunday observance, and the neighbours' opinion of them, all play their part in causing the tragedy and in heightening the bitterness of its effect. It is the social background the Poysers have provided for their niece and the standard of conduct imbibed from it that make it inevitable for Hetty to take flight before the birth of her baby; it is the esteem in which they are held by which the reader measures their shame and it is the clear sense he acquires of their identification with Hayslope by which he measures the anguish as well as the probability of their contemplated uprooting when the shame is known to them. Similarly, it is Arthur's upbringing, his relations with his grandfather, the squire, his high conception of the love and esteem he will earn from all his dependents when he inherits the land, that define the price he pays for his weakness. There is no part of what we have learnt of the outer circle that does not affect our sense of the inner. The cultured benignity of the rector, the moral enthusiasm of the Methodists, the simple ignorance of the country-folk, all make their own impact on the central characters and help to determine the events. Although the impression while we read is of a leisurely sequence of naturalistic scenes of comedy or of pathos and of a world richly populated with entertaining characters, when we look back we find that every individual scene or character is directly or indirectly related to the simple story at the core of the book, of the carpenter's betrothed betrayed by the squire's grandson. In its setting this commonplace story becomes widely significant. The simple, well-contrived pattern conveys the sense of a social structure enclosing four human beings as completely as the soil encloses the roots of a growing plant and, in so doing, it illustrates one aspect of the author's vision of life.

Although the formal pattern is not elsewhere so simple and symmetrical as it is in *Adam Bede*—where the assembly of the villagers on the green to hear the preaching in Book I, their assembly at the birthday feast in Book III and at the Harvest supper in Book VI provide rests that divide the composition into almost equal parts—the general character of the design, an individual tragedy surrounded by the life of a community, is similar in all George Eliot's novels, except *Daniel Deronda*, where the absence of such an enclosing community is an important part of her conception. In her own view the lack of symmetry in *The Mill on the Floss* was responsible for her imperfect fulfilment of her intention, and for the dissatisfaction that most readers feel about the end of that novel:

...the tragedy is not adequately prepared. This is a defect which I felt even while writing the third volume, and have felt ever since the MS. left me. The *Epische Breite* into which I was beguiled by love of my subject in the two first volumes, caused a want of proportionate fullness in the treatment of the third, which I shall always regret.[1]

The regret is justified in so far as the compression of the Maggie and Stephen episode contributes to its faulty presentation. Yet the epic breadth of the first two volumes is warranted by the completeness with which we come to understand the pressure of her surroundings on Maggie's developing personality which will, in turn, condition the central drama. We are brought to a full realization of those surroundings because, in a series of scenes, each with their own intrinsic value as social comedy, or drama, we grow familiar with a number of households and their way of life, which is both individual and representative. There is, for instance, the financially precarious home life of the Tullivers themselves; Mr Tulliver speculative, perplexed and, compared with his wife, adventurous, and Mrs Tulliver, foolish and faithful, torn between loyalty to her own family and to the proud conventions of her Dodson upbringing. Then there are the prosperous middle-class homes of her sisters; Mrs Glegg's home at St Ogg's with its 'front and back parlour so that she had two points of view from which she could observe the weakness of her fellow-beings, and reinforce her thankfulness for her own exceptional strength of mind', and the elegant home of Mrs Pullet with its 'front door mats by no means intended to wipe

[1] Cross, vol. II, p. 262; from a letter to Blackwood replying to the criticism of Sir Edward Bulwer Lytton.

shoes on: the very scraper had a deputy to do its dirty work'; and we are shown the well-conducted home life of Tom's ambitious clerical tutor, or, in contrast to all these, the home of Mr Tulliver's sister, Aunt Moss, who struggles to feed and clothe a large family on the proceeds of a farm starved of capital, since she has committed the indiscretion of marrying solely for love. All these aspects of life that the reader encounters as they impinge on Maggie's childhood, and that he relishes for their own vivid humour or pathos, convey the breadth of the world that surrounds an individual life and the narrowness of the space in which such a life can freely grow.

The difference in quality between George Eliot's novels is closely related to the degree of success with which she gives life to the social world surrounding her central characters. In her first period, from the *Scenes of Clerical Life* to *Silas Marner* she plants those characters in the environment with which she had been familiar since her childhood, and, for many readers, it is these novels that give the most delight. Certainly in them her characteristic humour, compounded of compassion, a sense of the incongruous, and an ear for dialogue that is both racy and individual, has the freest play. But when she returned, in *Middlemarch*, with a more assured command of her art, to the environment she most fully understood, she achieved her masterpiece. It is true that this great novel lacks some of the qualities of the first period; it has less spontaneous gaiety, partly because the provincial town gave her less scope for comedy than did the rural environment. There is also an aspect of her genius, absent here, which is more often found in the poet than in the prose artist, an ability to simplify without distorting human truths, so that they can be presented symbolically as they are in the legend of *Silas Marner*. The impulse towards such simplification is intrusive at the close of *The Mill on the Floss*, where the reunion in death of Maggie and Tom is out of key with the rest of the work and a similar discord between two modes of treatment distorts *Daniel Deronda*. But in *Silas Marner* the naturalistic treatment and the legendary story are happily combined and produce a minor masterpiece. Nevertheless, though certain excellencies must be sought elsewhere, *Middlemarch* is her widest and deepest study of the interpenetration between the life of a community and the individual lives that compose it.

The relative failure of *Romola*, *Felix Holt* and *Daniel Deronda* is partly due to the fact that in these three works, for different reasons, the social background is imperfectly focussed. In *Romola* this is the result of transplanting her scene to a world that she needed to reconstruct with laborious intellectual effort. In *Felix Holt*, although the ingredients of a first-rate George Eliot novel are all there, they are not successfully integrated. The romance of Esther and Felix usurps the foreground of the book and the more serious and interesting study of Mrs Transome and Jermyn, her son's father, is relegated to the background. The reader's interest oscillates between the political theme—the two contrasted radicals and their relations to the new voter—and the moral theme, illustrated by Mrs Transome reaping the fruits of her former self-indulgence and Esther moving towards her self-abnegating choice of true love and modest means. Because the various threads of interest do not compose into a single pattern *Felix Holt*, though enjoyable, does not enlarge the field of understanding as do the major novels. The social environment is not sufficiently convincing to provide a unifying centre; whereas, in the vintage works, the community has an identity as recognizable and persuasive as that of the central characters.

The case of *Daniel Deronda* is different. In this book the absence of an enveloping society for either Gwendolen or Daniel is a part of the author's central conception. Both characters are incomplete because they have been deprived of such a soil in which to grow. Gwendolen's selfishness and narrowness of vision and Daniel's quest for some communal tie to direct his altruistic aspirations are the outcome of a lack, in the early life of each, of just such a background as Hayslope provided for the characters in *Adam Bede*, the Dodson-Tulliver world for Maggie, or Middlemarch for Dorothea. George Eliot's perception of the dependence of human beings on one another and on their social and religious traditions is as keen in *Daniel Deronda* as elsewhere, but she attempts here to embody it by a process the reverse of the one she had mastered. Hitherto in her books the central drama had sprung from a tension between the individual and the community; she had posed her characters with the problem of adapting their personal desires, noble or selfish, to the inescapable surrounding conditions represented by an organic society. Her most characteristic gift was her power to embody those conditions and to frame her story within them. But in *Daniel Deronda* the social scenes, often vividly presented (for instance, the gambling scene; or the family life of the Cohens; or the archery party) are essentially disparate. They are of no service in fusing the themes into a single whole. Some incoherence in this last novel is due to the fact that the new approach presented a new problem in composition which was not successfully solved. The characteristic form of her novels is the product of a vision of life the source of which lay far back in her childhood. When she had found herself unable to accept the Christian dogmas she held fast to the ethical beliefs of which those dogmas had been the embodiment. She doubted the factual truth of the miraculous story told in the Gospels, and she doubted the factual truth of the theological dogma elicited from that story and developed in the tradition of the Church; but she had no doubt that human happiness and the full development of individual personality depend on mutual love and service. In 1848, eight years before she herself began to write fiction, and six years before she made her own moral choice to live with Lewes in defiance of the laws, conventions and religious teaching of the community, she commented on Charlotte Brontës treatment of Jane Eyre's problem:

All self-sacrifice is good, but one would like it to be in a somewhat nobler cause than that of diabolical law which chains a man soul and body to a putrefying carcase.[1]

The statement occurs in a letter to Charles Bray; the first clause, implying that self-sacrifice is good in itself would certainly have

[1] Cross, vol. 1, p. 191.

been modified later and might even then have been otherwise expressed if she had been writing more carefully than intimate correspondence requires. The conception of the good in self-sacrifice embodied in the novels is that it is relative and not absolute. Self-sacrifice is good because human happiness depends on it; man cannot live alone and social life is incompatible with unrestrained self-indulgence. This truth was most fully understood by her in relation to the English village and small town community life in which she had been bred, and in such communities, impregnated with social and religious traditions emerging in the conventions and observances of family and social life, it could be clearly illustrated. The problems which face Hetty and Arthur, Maggie and Stephen, Godfrey and Silas, Lydgate and Dorothea, are all problems concerned with the adjustment of the individual to the community, and with the discovery of a mean point between complete self-repression and unchecked self-indulgence. The motive for self-sacrifice is the happiness of other people and George Eliot composed her fictions in such a way as to set that motive in a clear light. But, by the time she wrote *Daniel Deronda*, she herself had long ceased to live in a community governed by traditions slowly evolved through centuries and unquestionably accepted by the majority. In the intellectual and artistic world in which she and George Henry Lewes were ultimately made welcome, there was no such tradition, woven of inherited beliefs, customs and conventions. Before she wrote *Daniel Deronda* she must have begun to ask herself how the law of mutual service and mutual deference to opinion operates for the *déraciné*. The unsatisfactory invention of Daniel's discovery of a Jewish allegiance and a mission to his people is an attempt to answer that question for him. It is not an intellectually satisfactory answer; nor has she successfully solved the artistic problem of linking the rootlessness of Daniel with the differently derived rootlessness of Gwendolen. The relationship between the two characters is potentially interesting, but they are arbitrarily brought together. Moreover, Daniel remains the symbol of an idea, whereas Gwendolen is the product of creative insight. The relative failure of the last novel is, in part, the failure to find an adequate substitute for that portrayal of a total society which gives her best novels their distinctive form.

The humour in George Eliot's novels, more prevalent in the earlier than in the later works, is as direct a product of her vision of life as is the way she shapes her stories. It arises out of a profound and sympathetic understanding of the world she creates and it expresses itself predominantly in the dialogue which bears the stamp both of the individual speaker and of the race and class. Behind the words spoken and the characteristic idiom lie the accumulated misconstructions of inherited beliefs, or the complex of prejudices, experience and common sense which make up rural wisdom. Mrs Poyser's gift for vivid self-expression, for instance, is more than a delightful idiosyncrasy. The metaphors that enrich her language spring from the soil in which she was nurtured. They reflect her own character and also the habits, the daily work, the religious tradition and the social conventions and assumptions of her time and class:

'I know there's them as is born t' own the land, and them as is born to sweat on't'—here Mrs Poyser paused to gasp a little—'and I know it's christened folks's duty to submit to their betters as fur as flesh and blood 'ull bear it; but I'll not make a martyr o' myself, and wear myself to skin and bone, and worret myself as if I was a churn wi' butter a-coming in't, for no landlord in England, not if he was King George himself.'[1]

The speech of George Eliot's rustic or provincial characters is racy because it represents personalities steeped in the history of the race. The variety of religious beliefs assimilated into the pieties and prejudices of the countryside is one aspect of this history and some of the humour in the novels arises out of consequent incongruities; for instance, Mrs Patten's shocked surprise, despite her regular church attendance, at being considered a 'miserable sinner':

'Eh, dear', said Mrs Patten, falling back in her chair, and lifting up her little withered hands, 'what 'ud Mr Gilfil say, if he was worthy to

[1] *Adam Bede*, bk. IV, ch. XXXII.

know the changes as have come about i' the Church these last ten years? I don't understand these new sort o' doctrines. When Mr Barton comes to see me, he talks about nothing but my sins and need o' marcy. Now, Mr Hackit, I've never been a sinner. From the fust beginning when I went into service I al'ys did my duty by my emplyers. I was a good wife as any in the county—never aggravated my husband. The cheese-factor used to say my cheese was al'ys to be depended on. I've known women, as their cheeses swelled a shame to be seen, when their husbands had counted on the cheese-money to make up their rent; and yet they'd three gowns to my one. If I'm not to be saved, I know many as are in a bad way.'[1]

Felix Holt's mother, a member of the General Baptist Connection, has a similar 'proper pride' in her own deserving:

... 'and as for being saved without works, there's a many, I daresay, can't do without that doctrine; but I thank the Lord I never needed to put *my*self on a level with the thief on the cross. I've done *my* duty and more, if anybody comes to that; for I've gone without my bit o' meat to make broth for a sick neighbour: and if there's any of the church members say they've done the same, I'd ask them if they had the sinking at the stomach as I have.'[2]

The author's attitude towards these women is not satirical. It is true that a sense of superior understanding contributes to the reader's enjoyment; but he is seldom allowed to feel contempt; and his amusement is often compatible with the reverse of this. He can, for instance, feel nothing but respect for Dolly Winthrop when she comes to help Silas with the baby and advocates baptism and ''noculation' as equivalent prophylactics against harm. Such confusions of thought are characteristic of rural life, and we are made to feel that Dolly Winthrop's human kindness is no less so. In the same novel the lucubrations of the philosophical Mr Macey evoke as much respect for his good sense as amusement over his elaborately imperfect logic. Mr Macey is, as clerk of the parish, well versed in the Prayer Book, but he interprets it in the light of his own experience and concludes that,

---

[1] *Scenes of Clerical Life, Amos Barton*, ch. I.   [2] *Felix Holt*, ch. IV.

if Silas Marner's knowledge of curative herbs owes something to the devil, no one, except the village doctor will be any the worse off for that. He offers consolation when Silas has lost his money:

'Come, Master Marner, why, you've no call to sit a-moaning. You're a deal better off to ha' lost your money, nor to ha' kep' it by foul means. I used to think, when you first come into these parts, as you were no better nor you should be; you were younger a deal than what you are now; but you were allays a staring, white-faced creatur, partly like a bald-faced calf, as I may say. But there's no knowing: it isn't every queer-looksed thing as Old Harry's had the making of—I mean, speaking o' toads and such; for they're often harmless, and useful against varmin. And it's pretty much the same wi' you, as fur as I can see. Though as to the yarbs and stuff to cure the breathing, if you brought that sort o' knowledge from distant parts, you might ha' been a bit freer of it. And if the knowledge wasn't well come by, why, you might ha' made up for it by coming to church reg'lar; for as for the children as the Wise Woman charmed, I've been at the christening of 'em again and again, and they took the water just as well. And that's reasonable; for if Old Harry's a mind to do a bit o' kindness for a holiday, like, who's got anything against it? That's my thinking; and I've been clerk o' this parish forty year, and I know, when the parson and me does the cussing of a Ash Wednesday, there's no cussing o' folks as have a mind to be cured without a doctor, let Kimble say what he will.'[1]

Social conventions provide a similar source of amusement, even the oddest of them are obviously accepted by their inheritors as a part of the order of nature. Moral and religious principles are not more binding than they are, nor are they indeed distinguishable from them. In this the Dodsons and the Tullivers are typical of their kind:

Their religion was of a simple, semi-pagan kind, but there was no heresy in it—if heresy properly means choice—for they didn't know there was any other religion, except that of chapel-goers, which appeared to run in families, like asthma. How *should* they know? The vicar of their pleasant rural parish was not a controversialist, but a good hand at whist, and one who had a joke always ready for a blooming

[1] *Silas Marner*, ch. x.

female parishioner. The religion of the Dodsons consisted in revering whatever was customary and respectable: it was necessary to be baptised, else one could not be buried in the churchyard, and to take the sacrament before death, as a security against more dimly understood perils; but it was of equal necessity to have the proper pall-bearers and well-cured hams at one's funeral, and to leave an unimpeachable will. A Dodson would not be taxed with the omission of anything that was becoming, or that belonged to that eternal fitness of things which was plainly indicated in the practice of the most substantial parishioners, and in the family traditions—such as obedience to parents, faithfulness to kindred, industry, rigid honesty, thrift, the thorough scouring of wooden and copper utensils, the hoarding of coins likely to disappear from the currency, the production of first-rate commodities for the market, and the general preference for whatever was home-made.[1]

This complex and inflexible Dodson code underlies the eccentricities of the individual sisters and permeates their behaviour at every turn of the story so that, delightfully surprising though they are, they are always recognizably in character.

The early books are necessarily richer in this humour arising out of intimacy with a tradition, since in them George Eliot is recreating the world in which she was born and bred. Yet even in *Daniel Deronda* there is an area in which her characteristic sense of comedy comes into play. The Cohen family are amusing and sympathetic in the same fashion as the Poysers or the Dodsons, and for the same reason. Their behaviour bears the stamp of race and tradition; and, as the reader gains intimacy with the Cohen family life, he respects and sympathizes with them while, at the same time, he relishes their incongruous mixture of generosity and greed, candour and cunning, moral rectitude and an eye for the main chance. The Cohens, like the Dodsons, have a streak of vulgarity—both families attach undue importance to their possessions as tokens of wealth and therefore of worth—but the Cohen vulgarities are specifically Jewish. Young Mrs Cohen wears 'a string of large artificial pearls wound round and round her neck', the baby sleeps under a scarlet counterpane and the

[1] *Mill on the Floss*, bk. IV, ch. I.

two children, Adelaide Rebekah and Jacob Alexander, are dressed respectively in braided amber and in 'black velveteen with scarlet stockings' when Daniel calls one afternoon at five o'clock. All this is as racial as is little Jacob's precocious sharpness over the transaction of 'shwopping' a corkscrew for Deronda's penknife with a white handle and a hook. No less so is the family affection and the pride of the grandmother and the mother in their offspring. But perhaps the quality of the Cohen family and the nature of the amusement they afford the reader can best be illustrated by the dialogue that takes place when Mordecai is to leave the household.—After Deronda had broken the news to the assembled family:

There was silence for a moment or two before the grandmother said in a wailing tone—

'Well, well! and so you're going away from us, Mordecai.'

'And where there's no children as there is here', said the mother, catching the wail.

'No Jacob, and no Adelaide, and no Eugenie!' wailed the grandmother again.

'Ay, ay, Jacob's learning 'ill all wear out of him. He must go to school. It'll be hard times for Jacob', said Cohen, in a tone of decision.[1]

Mordecai, in return for the Cohens' hospitality, has been teaching the boy. The accumulating sense of woe in the remarks of the family affects the children and the father's 'hard times for Jacob' is the last straw; Jacob sets up a wail, and his sister who 'always cried when her brother cried, now began to howl with astonishing suddenness, whereupon baby awaking contributed angry screams and required to be taken out of the cradle'. In this general turmoil Cohen,

...sensible that the master of the family must make some apology for all this weakness, and that the occasion called for a speech, addressed Deronda with some elevation of pitch, squaring his elbows and resting a hand on each knee:—

'It's not as we're the people to grudge anybody's good luck, sir, or the portion of their cup being made fuller, as I may say. I'm not an

[1] *Daniel Deronda*, bk. VI, ch. XLVI.

envious man, and if anybody offered to set up Mordecai in a shop of my sort two doors lower down, *I* shouldn't make wry faces about it. I'm not one of them that had need have a poor opinion of themselves, and be frightened at anybody else getting a chance. If I'm offal, let a wise man come and tell me, for I've never heard it yet. And in point of business, I'm not a class of goods to be in danger. If anybody takes to rolling me, I can pack myself up like a caterpillar, and find my feet when I'm let alone. And though, as I may say, you're taking some of our good works from us, which is a property bearing interest, I'm not saying but we can afford that, though my mother and my wife had the good will to wash and do for Mordecai to the last; and a Jew must not be like a servant who works for reward— though I see nothing against a reward if I can get it. And as to the extra outlay in schooling, I'm neither poor nor greedy—I wouldn't hang myself for sixpence, nor half a crown neither. But the truth of it is, the women and children are fond of Mordecai. You may partly see how it is, sir, by your own sense. A man is bound to thank God, as we do every Sabbath, that he was not made a woman; but a woman has to thank God that He has made her according to His will. And we all know what He has made her—a child-bearing, tender-hearted thing is the woman of our people. Her children are mostly stout, as I think you'll say Addy's are, and she's not mushy, but her heart is tender. So you must excuse present company, sir, for not being glad all at once....'[1]

The full flavour of this speech of Cohen's and its rich revelation of character is not the product of mere knowledge or of thought about racial characteristics. It is an imaginative recreation. George Eliot has identified herself with Cohen, so that she reproduces the cadence of his speech and the inconsequent twists and turns of his mind. He is self-assertive, acute, has an eye to the main chance (which includes earning the approval of his God). But he is also warm hearted, proud of the family he rules and not without dignity in his *apologia* for it. He is half ashamed (as a business man) and half proud (as a family man) to own that what really troubles them all in Mordecai's departure is not the loss of any profit, material or spiritual, but the loss of a friend they have grown to like.

[1] Ibid.

When Marian first considered writing fiction Lewes was confident that she had some of the requisite gifts while he was doubtful about others. The requirements he names indicate what the Victorian novelist was expected to provide, while the particular stamp of George Eliot's own talent reveals itself in the way the demands are met. The gifts that Lewes believes a novelist must have are philosophy, wit, descriptive powers and a sense of the dramatic which includes the ability to write dialogue and to achieve pathos. He was confident about the first three qualifications. 'You have wit, description, and philosophy—those go a good way towards the production of a novel'; but both he and she were doubtful whether she could 'write good dialogue' and whether she could 'command any pathos'. By the time *Amos Barton* was finished Lewes was satisfied about both. But, although her first story has humorous, character-revealing dialogue and gives evidence of an aural imagination which was to remain one of her notable gifts, the pathos of Milly's death does not ring true. The scene can still draw tears, as can many of Dickens's pathetic death-bed scenes, or indeed many screen plays of yet inferior quality. It is all too easy to draw tears by describing the death of a devoted mother who summons her children one by one to her bedside and harrows their feelings with her 'selfless' dying words. But such scenes are often, on reflection, unconvincing and few modern readers will be able to accept Milly's death-bed:

It seemed as if Milly had heard the little footsteps on the stairs, for when Amos entered her eyes were wide open, eagerly looking towards the door. They all stood by the bedside—Amos nearest to her, holding Chubby and Dickey. But she motioned for Patty to come first, and clasping the poor, pale child by the hand, said,—

'Patty, I'm going away from you. Love your Papa. Comfort him; and take care of your little brothers and sisters. God will help you.'

Patty stood perfectly quiet, and said, 'Yes, mamma.'

The mother motioned with her pallid lips for the dear child to lean towards her and kiss her; and then Patty's great anguish overcame her, and she burst into sobs. Amos drew her towards him, and pressed her head gently to him, while Milly beckoned Fred and Sophy, and said to them more faintly—

'Patty will try to be your mamma when I am gone, my darlings. You will be good and not vex her.'

They leaned towards her, and she stroked their fair heads, and kissed their tear-stained cheeks. They cried because mamma was ill and papa looked so unhappy; but they thought, perhaps next week things would be as they used to be again.

The little ones were lifted on the bed to kiss her. Little Walter said, 'Mamma, mamma', and stretched out his fat arms and smiled; and Chubby seemed gravely wondering; but Dickey, who had been looking fixedly at her, with lip hanging down, ever since he came into the room, now seemed suddenly pierced with the idea that Mamma was going away somewhere; his little heart swelled and he cried aloud.

Then Mrs Hackit and Nanny took them all away. Patty at first begged to stay at home and not go to Mrs Bond's again; but when Nanny reminded her that she had better go to take care of the younger ones, she submitted at once, and they were all packed in the pony-carriage once more.[1]

There is something radically wrong with this. The whole conception of a mother inflicting this memorable torture on her young family is unfortunate. If Victorian mothers really staged such theatrical death-bed scenes their notion of the seemly has dated. But one suspects that the scene is literary rather than naturalistic. In any case there is an over-emphasis on pathos in the style. Tear-provoking adjectives are over-worked; 'the *little* footsteps on the stairs', 'the *poor, pale* child', '*pallid* lips', 'the *dear* child', '*tear-stained* cheeks', 'his *little* heart'—the italicized adjectives are from the trading-stock of pathetic writing. And Milly's gasping last words that follow the exit of the children exhibit a sentimental self-indulgence which is out of character:

'My dear—dear—husband—you have been—very—good to me. You—have—made me—very—happy.'

He and she would both be well aware that he has not always been good to her and her dying fib could only turn the knife in the wound.

[1] *Scenes of Clerical Life*, Amos Barton, ch. VIII.

But though George Eliot's pathos was at first tainted with current literary fashion, or laid on too thick because of her mistrust of her powers in that line, she soon mastered the art of communicating her own sympathy with human suffering. The prison scene in *Adam Bede* when Dinah's passionate pity breaks down the barrier of bewildered bitterness that has kept Hetty silent, moves the reader far more deeply and lastingly than does Milly's death. This is of course partly because the experience of two-thirds of a long novel lies behind the scene. The reader has grown intimate with Hetty to an extent that he is never intimate with Milly and this achievement depends upon the fact that the author's 'dramatic power' preponderates over her 'wit' and her 'philosophy'—or rather transmutes these gifts—even in this first novel, in which the essayist's method is still at times too prominent. In the first half of the novel Hetty Sorrel is too often shown to the reader through the eyes of the author. Too often her moral and intellectual limitations are explained and her sensuous, kitten-like prettiness and selfishness demonstrated or reproved. But when the crisis comes George Eliot's creative genius takes command, and throughout the vivid scenes of Hetty's journey the reader becomes a participator in her misery instead of a superior person, merely measuring and pitying her moral and intellectual inadequacy. Hetty's loneliness and bewilderment, her self-sufficiency and dignity, her courage and her cowardice all emerge, without need of explanation, from what she does and says on the journey. We live through her long, difficult hours, borne up by the hope of finding Arthur at Windsor and share the bitterness and terror of her disappointment. And, when the land-lady at Windsor discovers Hetty's condition and feels her own superiority, George Eliot takes her stand with the reader at Hetty's side and glances satirically at the woman who is ready to cast the first stone:

'It 'ud have been a good deal better for her if she'd been uglier and had more conduct', said the landlady, who on any charitable con-struction must have been supposed to have more 'conduct' than beauty.

The reader lives with Hetty through the next stage of her wanderings, the 'Journey in Despair',[1] travelling vaguely towards Dinah, whom she will not reach, with the formed design of drowning herself, that she cannot accomplish. The scenes through which she passes are all seen through her eyes—the author's powers of description have become the servants of drama. When we part from Hetty at the end of that chapter our suspense and anxiety for her have obliterated all sense of moral superiority or separateness. And it is only after four chapters in which we share the feelings of those who are searching for her, that the end of the story is revealed. Consequently, the prison scene is no mere piece of pathetic writing, straining for the right emotional tone. It is the unfolding of the last scene of a drama we have watched with increasing participation. Sarah Stone, tobacconist at Stoniton who sheltered Hetty for the night and delivered the baby, has told her story at the trial. We have learnt how Hetty's inbred self-respect and dignity buoyed her up through that night and how, the next morning:

She would have no nay, but she would get up and be dressed, in spite of everything I could say. She said she felt quite strong enough; and it was wonderful what spirit she showed.

And we have shared Adam's experience when the woman tells the jury that Hetty went out with her baby:

The effect of this new evidence on Adam was electrical; it gave him new force. Hetty could not be guilty of the crime—her heart must have clung to her baby—else why should she have taken it with her?

But this hope in Adam is obliterated by the labourer's evidence, John Olding, who first heard the unexplained wailing as he went to fetch stakes after he had met Hetty 'looking white and scared'. When he came back to the spot an hour later he found the dead baby under a nut bush. And, as Olding gives his evidence, Adam learns the facts of the case and despairs: 'Hetty was guilty and he was silently calling on God to help'. Yet these are only

[1] *Adam Bede*, bk. v, ch. XXXVII.

facts. The real drama, the one that the reader by this time is concerned to understand, is the drama that took place in Hetty's soul. And this is unfolded, without comment, in Hetty's own halting words to Dinah in the prison. As we follow the exact sequence of Hetty's feelings we are lifted above the region of moral judgement; 'tout comprendre c'est tout pardonner'.

The wide scope of the novel form as it was used in the nineteenth century is the result of the combination of dramatic with narrative presentation. The reader accepts the convention of an omniscient narrator who knows all the motives and all the consequences of the action he describes and whose assessment of the values involved he is invited to share. But the total effect depends upon the tact and discrimination of the author in his use of the two methods. Intellectual appreciation of character can be arrived at by analysis; but for full sympathy we need to participate as well as to understand, and the quickening and expansion of sympathy was what George Eliot hoped to achieve in her novels:

> The only effect I ardently long to produce by my writings is, that those who read them should be better able to *imagine* and to *feel* the pains and the joys of those who differ from themselves in everything but the broad fact of being struggling, erring, human creatures.[1]

Sympathy for Hetty is almost choked by intellectual appreciation of her limitations and then, in the dramatic last scenes the 'broad fact' of our common humanity with her emerges. Even Tito Melema—who is in far greater danger of becoming merely a subject for speculation all the while the author dissects his character with relentless intelligence—evokes some fellow-feeling in dramatic scenes. The poverty of his nature and the gradual coarsening of his sensibility is not blurred—on the contrary it is particularly vivid when, for instance, he finds Baldassarre in Tessa's outhouse and hopes to propitiate him, or when he divulges to Romola the fact of his sale of her father's library. In both scenes the author's assessment of Tito's merits as

---

[1] Cross, vol. II, p. 118.

a human being is confirmed. But the reader's position is no longer merely that of a disinterested judge weighing the evidence. When we are allowed to watch the criminal in action and to overhear his thoughts, the predominant emotion is sympathy for his uncomprehending isolation. What emerges most clearly in these scenes is that Tito, for all his cleverness, is utterly at sea. His habit of selfish casuistry has made him incapable of foreseeing the impact of the situation on the straightforward upright mind of Baldassarre or of Romola. He expects a gesture of reconciliation, he expects sympathy or, at worst, forgiveness, and his alarmed discovery of his loneliness extends the reader's capacity for sympathy.

In these cases dramatic presentation redresses or nearly redresses a balance. Analysis preponderates in the drawing of Hetty and Tito so as almost to defeat the author's declared intention. In the later books, however, the unlovely characters are seldom allowed to become mere case histories, coldly appraised by the reader with the help of the author's intellectual analysis. The reader is not invited to feel merely judicial about Casaubon, or Mrs Transome or Gwendolen Harleth. There are scenes enough in which we are given their thoughts and speech at a crisis. Dramatic presentation alone can be trusted to elicit the response 'there, but for the grace of God, go I'; but by dramatic presentation that response can be evoked even for the characters the reader least believes himself to resemble. Such presentation may take the form of dialogue (Dorothea and Casaubon mutually attempting to communicate and misunderstanding one another's purposes) or it may take the form of a more violent clash, a dramatic crisis such as in the theatre produces the moment of highest tension. Big scenes of this kind were included in the novelist's business in the nineteenth century. They were an expected part of the entertainment. In her first experiment with the traditional form of prose narrative George Eliot laid on her dramatic scenes as she laid on her pathos. She was as yet only fumbling towards the expression of her personal vision of life. In the presentation of *The Sad Fortunes of the*

Rev. Amos Barton, along with the relatively assured recreation of a social background and the naturalistic portrait of Amos himself, including the characteristic effort to obtain the reader's sympathy for this ungainly, egoistic and intellectually limited human being, there is the contrived pathos of Milly's death. In *Mr Gilfil's Love Story* there is contrived dramatic (or melodramatic) excitement. The scene in which Caterina goes out to murder her faithless lover, and finds him lying dead in the wood, does not succeed in being more than that. It is written in the style of crude melodrama, the present tense is used to heighten excitement and histrionic similes are liberally interspersed to evoke a mood of expectant horror:

See how she rushes noiselessly, like a pale meteor, along the passages and up the gallery stairs! Those gleaming eyes, those bloodless lips, that swift silent tread, make her look like the incarnation of a fierce purpose, rather than a woman. The midday sun is shining on the armour in the gallery, making mimic suns on bossed sword-hilts and the angles of polished breast-plates. Yes, there are sharp weapons in the gallery. There is a dagger in that cabinet; she knows it well. And as a dragon-fly wheels in its flight to alight for an instant on a leaf, she darts to the cabinet, takes out the dagger, and thrusts it into her pocket.[1]

That, and almost all that follows to the end of the chapter, might come from any sensational magazine story. And when George Eliot tries, by direct intervention, to persuade her reader to accept Caterina as a real human being, the reader remains detached, interested only—if interested at all—to know what happened next:

Poor child! poor child! she who used to cry to have the fish put back into the water—who never willingly killed the smallest living thing—dreams now, in the madness of her passion, that she can kill the man whose very voice unnerves her.[2]

But in the later novels, though certain scenes and situations are no less abnormal than Caterina's, the interest is focussed throughout on the mind and spirit of the protagonist. It does not matter whether Bulstrode was responsible for Raffles's death (in *Middlemarch*) or Gwendolen for Grandcourt's (in *Daniel Deronda*); what

[1] *Scenes of Clerical Life, Mr Gilfil's Love Story*, ch. XIII. [2] Ibid.

concerns us is what occurs in the mind of each. Each of them wills the death of a fellow-creature and in each case the dramatic tension is the result of the conflict in their minds which the reader witnesses through its whole evolution, before and after the death takes place. The physical cause of death, which would concern a court of law, is as irrelevant as is the cause of the death of the wife of T. S. Eliot's hero in *The Family Reunion*. And, in consequence of focussing the interest on the mind of her protagonist, George Eliot succeeds in these dramatic moments in doing what she failed to do with Caterina. The reader participates in the will to murder; his power of understanding and sympathy is stretched far enough to include that, and the total effect of the ensuing death on the mind of the would-be murderer. Moreover, because the author is wholly engaged in the act of creation—that is in participating imaginatively in the experience she presents— she is not lured into any literary clichés or exaggerations of style; the situation develops naturally towards its crisis. The quiet statement:

Bulstrode had not yet unravelled in his thought the confused promptings of the last four and twenty hours.

is significant because we have lived through those hours. When the moment comes in which the suspicions of the neighbours culminate in Bulstrode's public disgrace it is again not so much what happens that holds the reader spell-bound, but the reverberations of every act and speech in the minds of Bulstrode and Lydgate. Grandcourt's death scene is not so securely handled as Raffles's. In *Middlemarch* George Eliot is writing in a form she had completely mastered and this dramatic crisis is controlled by the whole pattern of the book, its total effect depends upon the world in which it occurs and the reader's response to the particular scenes of the 'murder' or of the public disgrace are involved with his total response to the novel. The relative failure of *Daniel Deronda* as a whole reflects itself in the crisis; we arrive at the central moment of Grandcourt's drowning in the scene in which Gwendolen confesses herself to Deronda and that scene suffers

7-2

from the fact that Deronda himself is never wholly convincing. In the actual writing of this scene there are signs that the author is distracted from her imaginative reconstruction of Gwendolen's experience by her effort to persuade us of Deronda's reality. Nevertheless, Gwendolen's own words evoke the pith of her experience:

'I know nothing—I only know that I saw my wish outside me.'...

'I was leaping from my crime, and there it was—close to me as I fell—there was the dead face—dead, dead. It can never be altered. That was what happened. That was what I did. You know it all. It can never be altered.' [1]

George Eliot's novels have in them all the elements expected by nineteenth-century novel readers. They were written within the tradition and she proved to have all the talents that Lewes knew she would need if she was to succeed in the genre. From one point of view her novels continue in the tradition evolved from Fielding, but which had gradually become less picaresque and more strictly narrative. She tells a story with a beginning, middle and end. The main interest is focussed on a small group of characters the development of whose fortunes is laid out. They move towards a crisis or tangle which is unravelled before the end so that in the last chapter a *dénouement* is reached. All the fortunes with which the reader has been concerned are tidied up. The story ends in a marriage or a death and the future of the survivors is indicated. The reader is persuaded that the story is complete. Within this framework there is scope for the narrator to comment on the action and the characters and so to expound his 'philosophy' or sense of moral values. 'Wit', both in the commentary and in the dialogue, contributes to the reader's delight and communicates the author's sense of proportion; 'descriptive powers' evoke the surroundings in which the action takes place, while 'dramatic powers' enable the author to recreate the scenes of the story in terms of dialogue and action. But from another point of view George Eliot is an innovator. The organic or living form of her novels, within the expected framework, is

[1] *Daniel Deronda*, bk. VII, ch. LVI.

different from anything that had gone before. It resembles, in some respects, Jane Austen's form in so far as the central characters are deeply rooted in their social environment which determines their story as much as does their individual character. The difference is that the social environment is wider, more complex, made up of a greater variety of minor characters drawn from many more social and economic levels, and also that the display of this outer circle or environment is more conscious. Jane Austen took her social *milieu* for granted; its manners and traditions were, for her, as little open to question as the laws of nature. George Eliot was aware of the ethical, religious and social conventions of the world she paints as a product of history, evolved in time and changing with time. She was consciously interested in the pressure all these exert on individual lives and in the existence of a problem concerned with resisting or succumbing to that pressure. She shares the modern consciousness of man in a changing and developing society. Consequently, the organic form of her novels—an inner circle (a small group of individuals involved in a moral dilemma) surrounded by an outer circle (the social world within which the dilemma has to be resolved)—is more significant than in any preceding fiction. Furthermore, her perception of individual human beings is more complex than that of her predecessors. She never suggests a simple division of characters into good and bad. The individual, like the environment, has evolved and is evolving; his or her behaviour at any given moment is the inevitable result of all that has gone before; therefore, while the action can itself be judged, both in relation to its consequences and to its aesthetic beauty (an action that pleases or displeases) the doer is not presented judicially but compassionately. In her discourse George Eliot sometimes deviates from this attitude and her novel suffers accordingly. But whenever her reflective powers are in due subordination to her creative gift, wherever, as usually happens in the dialogue, she responds to her characters rather than thinks about them, the reader feels with them and the total effect of her novel is an increase of understanding and of compassion.

CHAPTER V

ADAM BEDE

IN *Adam Bede*, published in 1859, George Eliot gave herself for the first time the wide canvas of the three-volume novel. The first intention was that it should be published serially in *Blackwood's Magazine* and the reversal of that decision may well have enabled her to develop her subject with more regard for the total form than was customary in piecemeal publication. George Eliot's own account of the inception and the growth of the book gives us some clues about its composition; but she was not consciously interested in form and neither she, nor any other novelist of her day, discusses the shape of a novel with alert awareness comparable to what we find in Henry James's prefaces. The organization of material was a more or less unconscious result of her conception of the subject. When she reflects about her work and describes its development in her journal, she writes about characters, scenes, story and moral content, and not about the disposition of the parts. The entry in the journal for 16 November 1858, when she has just written the last word of the novel, indicates the degree in which the characters of Adam and Dinah were drawn from life, and reveals the problems of composition of which the author was most clearly aware.

Nov. 16 (1858).—Wrote the last word of 'Adam Bede' and sent it to Mr Langford. *Jubilate*.

The germ of 'Adam Bede' was an anecdote told me by my Methodist Aunt Samuel (the wife of my father's younger brother),—an anecdote from her own experience. We were sitting together one afternoon during her visit to me at Griff, probably in 1839 or 1840, when it occurred to her to tell me how she had visited a condemned criminal,— a very ignorant girl, who had murdered her child and refused to confess; how she had stayed with her praying through the night, and how the poor creature at last broke out into tears, and confessed her crime. My aunt afterwards went with her in the cart to the place of execution; and she described to me the great respect with which this ministry of hers was regarded by the official people about the gaol. The story, told by my aunt with great feeling, affected me deeply, and I never lost the impression of that afternoon and our talk together; but I believe I never mentioned it, through all the intervening years, till something prompted me to tell it to George in December 1856, when I had begun to write the 'Scenes of Clerical Life'. He remarked that the scene in the prison would make a fine element in a story; and I afterwards began to think of blending this and some other recollections of my aunt in one story, with some points in my father's early life and character. The problem of construction that remained was to make the unhappy girl one of the chief *dramatis personae*, and connect her with the hero. At first I thought of making the story one of the series of 'Scenes', but afterwards, when several motives had induced me to close these with 'Janet's Repentance', I determined on making what we always called in our conversation 'My Aunt's Story' the subject of a long novel, which I accordingly began to write on the 22nd October 1857.

The character of Dinah grew out of my recollections of my aunt, but Dinah is not at all like my aunt, who was a very small, black-eyed woman, and (as I was told, for I never heard her preach) very vehement in her style of preaching. She had left off preaching when I knew her, being probably sixty years old, and in delicate health; and she had become, as my father told me, much more gentle and subdued than she had been in the days of her active ministry and bodily strength, when she could not rest without exhorting and remonstrating, in season and out of season. I was very fond of her, and enjoyed the few weeks of her stay with me greatly. She was loving and kind to me, and I could talk to her about my inward life, which was closely shut up from those usually round me. I saw her only twice again, for much shorter periods,—once at her own home at Wirksworth in Derbyshire, and once at my father's last residence, Foleshill.

The character of Adam and one or two incidents connected with him were suggested by my father's early life; but Adam is not my father any more than Dinah is my aunt. Indeed, there is not a single portrait in 'Adam Bede'; only the suggestions of experience wrought up into new combinations. When I began to write it, the only elements I had determined on, besides the character of Dinah, were the character of Adam, his relation to Arthur Donnithorne, and their mutual relations to Hetty—i.e. to the girl who commits child-murder,—the scene in the prison being, of course, the climax towards which I worked. Everything else grew out of the characters and their mutual relations. Dinah's ultimate relation to Adam was suggested by George, when I had read to him the first part of the first volume; he was so delighted with the presentation of Dinah, and so convinced that the reader's interest would centre in her, that he wanted her to be the principal figure at the last. I accepted the idea at once, and from the end of the third chapter worked with it constantly in view.

The first volume was written at Richmond, and given to Blackwood in March. He expressed great admiration of its freshness and vividness, but seemed to hesitate about putting it in the Magazine, which was the form of publication he, as well as myself, had previously contemplated. He still *wished* to have it for the Magazine, but desired to know the course of the story....I refused to tell my story beforehand, on the ground that I would not have it judged apart from my *treatment*, which alone determines the moral quality of art; and ultimately I proposed that the notion of publication in 'Maga' should be given up, and that the novel should be published in three volumes at Christmas, if possible. He assented....

Work was slow and interrupted at Munich, and when we left I had only written to the beginning of the dance on the birthday feast; but at Dresden I wrote uninterruptedly, and with great enjoyment in the long, quiet mornings, and there I nearly finished the second volume—all, I think, but the last chapter, which I wrote here in the old room at Richmond in the first week of September, and then sent the MS. off to Blackwood. The opening of the third volume—Hetty's journey—was, I think, written more rapidly than the rest of the book, and was left without the slightest alteration of the first draught. Throughout the book I have altered little; and the only cases I think in which George suggested more than a verbal alteration, when I read the MS. aloud to him, were the first scene at the farm, and the scene in the wood between Arthur and Adam, both of which he recommended me to space out a little, which I did.

When, on October 29, I had written to the end of the love scene at the farm, between Adam and Dinah, I sent the MS. to Blackwood, since the remainder of the third volume could not affect the judgement on what had gone before. He wrote back in warm admiration, and offered me, on the part of the firm, £800 for four years' copyright. I accepted the offer. The last words of the third volume were written and despatched on their way to Edinburgh, November the 16th, and now on the last day of the same month I have written this slight history of my book. I love it very much, and am deeply grateful to have written it, whatever the public may say of it—a result which is still in darkness, for I have at present had only four sheets of the proof.[1]

In her own account it appears that the problem of construction presented itself as the necessity to integrate the story of Adam with that of Hetty and Dinah. Arthur's and Adam's relation to each other and to Hetty provide the link and the marriage between Dinah and Adam (suggested by Lewes) rounds off the whole and satisfies contemporary conventions by linking the lives of the hero and heroine at the close.

But in the composition of the novel George Eliot achieved an artistic triumph of which she was only partially conscious. She 'loved the book', which implies that she was satisfied that some part of her vision of life was communicated in it. But she was more aware of having overcome certain difficulties in weaving the narrative than of how she had, instinctively, set the story of a few individuals in due relation to the environment from which they sprang. On the other hand, she was also unaware that there are certain weaknesses in her presentation of the subject which interfere at times with the reader's apprehension of it. The principal defect of this kind is that the didactic essays, explaining the characters or the moral import of their stories, are too long and of too frequent occurrence. Later novelists have succeeded in eliminating this element altogether; but in the eighteen-fifties they were a traditional part of the art of fiction. The manner had been inaugurated by Fielding, and Thackeray perpetuated it in the nineteenth century, especially in *Vanity Fair*. In 1857 George Eliot wrote of Thackeray:

I am not conscious of being in any way a disciple of his, unless it constitute discipleship to think him, as I suppose the majority of people with any intellect do, on the whole the most powerful of living novelists.[2]

[1] Cross, vol. ii, pp. 65 ff.   [2] Ibid., vol. i, p. 461.

She is not a disciple in so far as her outlook and her material are radically different. Moreover, the predominantly satiric intention of *Vanity Fair* is totally unlike her own predominantly compassionate intention. It is essential to her effect that the reader should fully participate in the lives of her characters and identify himself as closely as possible with them. Thackeray, on the contrary, in *Vanity Fair* invites and suggests detached observation and critical amusement at the expense of his worldlings. He makes use of the essay to establish himself as showman and to create a relation between himself and the reader which serves his purpose. It was unfortunate, though it was also natural, that George Eliot should, in her first novel, accept a method of presentation that was current and that was used by the author she most admired. Her manner of using the asides to the reader is also partly the result of distrust in her own creative power. She is not convinced that the fruits of her imagination will convey to the reader all that her own intelligence discerns. So, from time to time, she breaks the illusion that she has so successfully built up, the illusion that we are actually in Hayslope, becoming intimate with its society and discovering the tragic situation of Hetty, Arthur and Adam as it gradually unfolds itself. She reminds us that we are merely reading a story of which she is the narrator and she lets us know that she suspects us of being incapable of understanding the experience she has been at pains to give us. An extreme example of this defect occurs in the first chapter of Book II, which is characteristically entitled 'In which the story pauses a little'. In it she makes a wholly unnecessary apology for painting the Rector of Broxton, Mr Irwine, as a very pleasant man and not a saint and she discourses at unnecessary length about her own artistic aims. It is unnecessary, because those aims reveal themselves in their achievement. The chapter opens with an account of the average incumbents of country parishes in 1799, and continues:

So I am content to tell my simple story, without trying to make things seem better than they were; dreading nothing, indeed, but falsity, which, in spite of one's best efforts, there is reason to dread.

Falsehood is so easy, truth so difficult. The pencil is conscious of a delightful facility in drawing a griffin—the longer the claws, and the larger the wings, the better; but that marvellous facility which we mistook for genius is apt to forsake us when we want to draw a real unexaggerated lion. Examine your words well, and you will find that even when you have no motive to be false, it is a very hard thing to say the exact truth, even about your own immediate feelings—much harder than to say something fine about them which is *not* the exact truth.

It is for this rare, precious quality of truthfulness that I delight in many Dutch paintings, which lofty-minded people despise. I find a source of delicious sympathy in these faithful pictures of a monotonous homely existence, which has been the fate of so many more among my fellow-mortals than a life of pomp or of absolute indigence, of tragic suffering or of world-stirring actions.

The essay goes on for seven pages before she returns to Mr Irwine, its occasion 'with whom I desire you to be in perfect charity, far as he may be from satisfying your demands on the clerical character'. If we adopt what Matthew Arnold calls 'the historical estimate' this intrusion of discourse can be accepted. It is there because that mode conforms to contemporary tradition in novel-writing, and because there was evidently still some reluctance among publisher's readers if not among the critics or the general public, to accept naturalistic characters and situations in fiction. But if we judge by the effect on our total experience of the book these essays are detrimental. They often contain matter which seems platitudinous to the modern reader and at best they interrupt the narrative and set it at a distance. Moreover, most readers of *Adam Bede*, far from complaining that the characters are 'not altogether handsome' have objected, at any rate to two of them, on the grounds that they are too handsome.

Both Adam and Dinah are found too virtuous by some modern readers. The charge may mean that they are too virtuous to be credible, or that they are too virtuous to be sympathetic. In either case Adam and Dinah cannot properly be discussed as though the author treated them alike. If both are unsatisfactory, it is for different reasons. In my own opinion the objection to Adam is the result of misunderstanding. Dinah is presented without a fault, but Adam is not. Yet it is doubtful whether her faultlessness is the real reason why she does not always command sympathy. Other saintly characters in fiction succeed in doing so, for instance Dostoyevski's Alyosha in *The Brothers Karamazov* or Prince Myshkin in *The Idiot*. And Dinah herself becomes more sympathetic in Book VI, not because she is less faultless, but because the author allows us to discern her human nature more clearly when she blushes and trembles at Adam's voice, when she resists him in case her love for the creature should interfere with her devotion to the Creator, and when she finally submits. If the characterization of Dinah partially fails to produce the effect intended, it is not because she is too virtuous but because of the author's treatment of her subject. It is in part because she intervenes too much, explicitly guiding the reader's response by her own comments, and it is in part the result of Dinah's semi-biblical idiom. Doubtless that idiom is a faithful record of the speech of Aunt Samuel and other Methodists, but it is none the less a self-conscious and irritating mode of speech. When Dinah's conversation is set beside Lisbeth Bede's in a scene in which George Eliot's excellent ear for dialogue probably catches the tune of each with equal fidelity, Lisbeth sounds natural and wins the reader's sympathy, whereas Dinah sounds priggish and stilted. The scene occurs when Dinah visits Mrs Bede to try and comfort her after the death of her husband. Dinah enters quietly and, for a moment, Lisbeth thinks she is some spirit. But Dinah lays her hand upon her, and Lisbeth recognizes the work-scarred hand of one of her own kind:

'Why, ye're a workin' woman!'

'Yes, I am Dinah Morris, and I work in the cotton-mill when I am at home.'

'Ah!' said Lisbeth slowly, still wondering; 'ye comed in so light, like the shadow on the wall, an' spoke i' my ear, as I thought ye might be a sperrit. Ye've got a'most the face o' one as is a-sittin' on the grave i' Adam's new Bible.'

'I come from the Hall Farm now. You know Mrs Poyser—she's

my aunt, and she has heard of your great affliction, and is very sorry; and I'm come to see if I can be any help to you in your trouble; for I know your sons Adam and Seth, and I know you have no daughter; and when the clergyman told me how the hand of God was heavy upon you, my heart went out towards you, and I felt a command to come and be to you in the place of a daughter in this grief, if you will let me.'

'Ah! I know who y' are now; y' are a Methody, like Seth; he's tould me on you', said Lisbeth, fretfully, her overpowering sense of pain returning, now her wonder was gone. 'Ye'll make it out as trouble's a good thing, like *he* allays does. But where's the use o' talkin' to me a-that'n? Ye canna make the smart less wi' talkin'. Ye'll ne'er make me believe as its better for me not to ha' my old man die in's bed, if he must die, an ha' the parson to pray by him, an' me to sit by him, an' tell him ne'er to mind th' ill words I've gi'en him sometimes when I war angered, an' to gi' him a bit an' a sup, as long as a bit an' a sup he'd swallow. But eh! to die i' the cold water, an' us close to him, an ne'er to know; an me a-sleepin', as if I ne'er belonged to him no more nor if he'd been a journeyman tramp from nobody knows where!'

Here Lisbeth began to cry and rock herself again; and Dinah said—

'Yes, dear friend, your affliction is great. It would be hardness of heart to say that your trouble was not heavy to bear. God didn't send me to you to make light of your sorrow, but to mourn with you, if you will let me. If you had a table spread for a feast, and was making merry with your friends, you would think it was kind to let me come and rejoice with you, because you'd think I should like to share those good things; but I should like better to share in your trouble and labour, and it would seem harder to me if you denied me that. You won't send me away? You're not angry with me for coming?' [1]

There is a distasteful over-carefulness about Dinah's idiom. The consciousness of virtue, hard to distinguish from self-righteousness, that Dinah's speeches betray is an obstacle to sympathy from which Alyosha and Myshkin are free; but it is not George Eliot's intention to burden Dinah with self-conscious virtue. With Adam the case is different. It is evident that the author intended self-righteousness to be the flaw in his character which is partially if not wholly purged by the suffering he undergoes

---

[1] *Adam Bede*, bk. I, ch. x.

GEORGE ELIOT

in the course of the story. Adam, before the tragic climax in the prison, is a prig and forfeits some of the reader's sympathy in consequence. But the author deliberately draws him as a man who is too apt to moralize on all occasions. When Arthur Donnithorne, long before the rift in their friendship, speaks of the probability that Burge will take Adam into partnership adding 'He will, if he is wise', Adam cannot forgo the opportunity to preach:

'Nay, sir, I don't see as he'd be much the better off for that. A foreman, if he's got a conscience, and delights in his work, will do his business as well as if he was a partner. I wouldn't give a penny for a man as 'ud drive a nail in slack because he didn't get extra pay for it.'[1]

Similarly, he preaches to his mother when she nags at him for putting on his best clothes to visit Hetty:

'Nay, nay, mother', said Adam, gravely, and standing still while he put his arm on her shoulder, 'I'm not angered. But I wish, for thy own sake, thee'dst be more contented to let me do what I've made up my mind to do. I'll never be no other than a good son to thee as long as we live. But a man has other feelings besides what he owes to's father and mother; and thee oughtna to want to rule over me body and soul. And thee must make up thy mind, as I'll not give way to thee where I've a right to do what I like. So let us have no more words about it.'[2]

This gratuitous didacticism is a part of George Eliot's conception of Adam's character. The reader who feels respect for Adam from the first, but only a limited liking, is being affected as she meant that he should be. The proof of this is that she allows Adam finally to discover, as the result of suffering, that his own self-righteousness had marred his relation to his father and mother, to Arthur Donnithorne, and even to Hetty. His acute suffering 'alone in his dull upper room' outside the prison in which Hetty awaits her trial is mingled with mortification. It is there that he first begins to recognize his own failings.

[1] *Adam Bede*, bk. I, ch. XVI.
[2] Ibid., bk. II, ch. XX.

The second scene with Arthur in the wood, in which the reconciliation takes place, is the penultimate scene of his self-discovery and purgation. The behaviour of both men is convincing throughout the scene and the obstacles, inherent in the nature of each, are very gradually overcome until at last, after a silence of several minutes, Adam says:

'It's true what you say, sir: I'm hard—it's in my nature. I was too hard with my father, for doing wrong. I've been a bit hard t' every-body but *her*. I felt as if nobody pitied her enough—her suffering cut into me so; and when I thought the folks at the Farm were too hard on her, I said I'd never be hard to anybody myself again. But feeling over-much about her has perhaps made me unfair to you. I've known what it is in my life to repent and feel it's too late: I felt I'd been too harsh to my father when he was gone from me—I feel it now, when I think of him. I've no right to be hard towards them as have done wrong and repent.'[1]

Finally, when Adam discovers his love for Dinah, he sees in a full light what has been amiss in himself:

'It's like as if it was a new strength to me', he said to himself, 'to love her, and know as she loves me. I shall look t' her to help me to see things right. For she's better than I am—there's less o' self in her, and pride. And it's a feeling as gives you a sort o' liberty, as if you could walk more fearless, when you've more trust in another than y'have in yourself. I've always been thinking I knew better than them as belonged to me, and that's a poor sort o' life, when you can't look to them nearest to you t'help you with a bit better thought than what you've got inside you a'ready.'[2]

The marriage of Dinah and Adam is justified as a part of the composition, if for no other reason, because it enables the author to put this last touch to her definition of Adam's character. When George Eliot chose for her novel her aunt's story of a country girl, seduced by a young squire and charged with the murder of her baby, her first task was to imagine the thoughts and feelings of the pair throughout. She makes the reader accept the

[1] *Ibid.*, bk. v, ch. XLVIII.   [2] *Ibid.*, bk. VI, ch. LIV.

tragedy as the seemingly inevitable outcome of their characters and circumstances. Both characters are developed with intelligent sympathy and thoroughness and everything is done to make the reader understand their predicament and the degree in which each is responsible for all that ensues. George Eliot portrays with insight and convincing truth Hetty's physical charms and her shallow, pleasure-loving, heartless nature, without ill-will but without any strength of purpose to withstand temptation. And she analyses Arthur's character, generous, impulsive, greedy for the approval of his fellows but prone to yield to his own immediate desires and to trust the future to take care of itself. We know them both partly by the effect they produce upon those around them; by the fascination Hetty exercises, not only over Arthur and Adam, but even over her shrewd aunt, Mrs Poyser, who

...continually gazed at Hetty's charms by the sly, fascinated in spite of herself; and after administering such a scolding as naturally flowed from her anxiety to do well by her husband's niece—who had no mother of her own to scold her, poor thing!—she would often confess to her husband, when they were safe out of hearing, that she firmly believed, 'the naughtier the little huzzy behaved, the prettier she looked'.[1]

The only one who perceives from the first a dangerous lack in Hetty's equipment for life is Dinah, who yearns over

...that sweet young thing, with life and all its trials before her—the solemn daily duties of the wife and mother—and her mind so unprepared for them all; bent merely on little, foolish, selfish pleasures, like a child hugging its toys in the beginning of a long toilsome journey, in which it will have to bear hunger and cold and unsheltered darkness.[2]

We know Hetty and Arthur also by their actions and their speech, by Arthur's behaviour to his grandfather, to his tenants or to Mr Irwine, by Hetty's behaviour to her uncle and aunt, to their children or to Adam. And we are given their private thoughts in which their motives are laid bare. In addition to all

---

[1] *Adam Bede*, bk. I, ch. VII.   [2] Ibid., bk. I, ch. XV.

this there is much—indeed too much—of the author's choral commentary. Sometimes there are heavily ironical asides about such enchantingly pretty women as Hetty; such as:

Ah, what a prize the man gets who wins a sweet bride like Hetty! How the men envy him who come to the wedding breakfast, and see her hanging on his arm in her white lace and orange blossoms. The dear, young, round, soft, flexible thing! Her heart must be just as soft, her temper just as free from angles, her character just as pliant. If anything ever goes wrong, it must be the husband's fault there: he can make her what he likes—that is plain. And the lover himself thinks so too: the little darling is so fond of him, her little vanities are so bewitching, he wouldn't consent to her being a bit wiser; those kitten-like glances and movements are just what one wants to make one's hearth a paradise. Every man under such circumstances is conscious of being a great physiognomist. Nature, he knows, has a language of her own, which she uses with strict veracity, and he considers himself an adept in the language. Nature has written out his bride's character for him in those exquisite lines of cheek and lip and chin, in those eyelids delicate as petals, in those long lashes curled like the stamen of a flower, in the dark liquid depths of those wonderful eyes. How she will dote on her children! She is almost a child herself, and the little pink round things will hang about her like florets round the central flower; and the husband will look on, smiling benignly, able, whenever he chooses, to withdraw into the sanctuary of his wisdom, towards which his sweet wife will look reverently, and never lift the curtain. It is a marriage such as they made in the golden age, when the men were all wise and majestic, and the women all lovely and loving.

It was very much in this way that our friend Adam Bede thought about Hetty; only he put his thoughts into different words....[1]

Sometimes there is an essay discoursing with scrupulous justice and clear intelligence about the insidious development of weakness into self-justifying wickedness in such men as Arthur:

Our deeds determine us, as much as we determine our deeds; and until we know what has been or will be the peculiar combination of outward with inward facts, which constitutes a man's critical actions, it will be better not to think ourselves wise about his character. There

[1] Ibid.

is a terrible coercion in our deeds which may first turn the honest man into a deceiver, and then reconcile him to the change; for this reason—that the second wrong presents itself to him in the guise of the only practicable right. The action which before commission has been seen with that blended common sense and fresh untarnished feeling which is the healthy eye of the soul, is looked at afterwards with the lens of apologetic ingenuity, through which all things that men call beautiful and ugly are seen to be made up of textures very much alike. Europe adjusts itself to a *fait accompli*, and so does an individual character,—until the placid adjustment is disturbed by a convulsive retribution.[1]

The total effect of the careful characterization of Arthur and Hetty is that we understand them, are convinced of the truth of the author's analysis, and yet we hardly ever identify ourselves with them. The distance that lies between them and their author, bridged only by intellectual understanding and by compassion, reproduces itself as a similar distance between them and the reader. We know them better than we know Mr Irwine because their story concerns us more and at certain moments its pitch rises to great dramatic intensity. Nevertheless, they suffer in some degree as Mr Irwine does from being over-explained. The rector becomes a picturesque historical reconstruction rather than a living personality and Arthur and Hetty tend to become exemplars or symbolic figures illustrating important moral truths.

In this first novel the gap between the artist and the thinker is too often perceptible. George Eliot's width of thought, her intelligence and her serious concern with ethical problems were assets; but before they could enrich her novels she had to make her ideas (to use her own phrase), 'thoroughly incarnate'. Their validity for the reader, even their interest, depends upon his discovering them for himself as he watches the interplay of character and event. Too often in *Adam Bede* the reader is not in direct contact with the action—the author intervenes to direct his judgement. But both the insight of the directing mind and the imaginative power of the rare moments when it is silent give promise of what was to come.

[1] *Adam Bede*, bk. IV, ch. XXIX.

CHAPTER VI

THE MILL ON THE FLOSS

IN 1860, one year after *Adam Bede* and a short story called *The Lifted Veil*, Blackwood published George Eliot's second full-length novel, *The Mill on the Floss*. Both the greater strength and the greater weakness of this novel compared with the first arise out of a new element in it, the element of autobiography. George Eliot is identified with Maggie Tulliver in a different way and to a different degree from that in which she is identified with any character in *Adam Bede*. Her intimacy with the feelings and development of the child Maggie give a new depth to the book and to the other characters who dominate the first part. Mr and Mrs Tulliver, Tom, and the aunts have a peculiar vitality, the outcome of a child's memories focussed and selected by mature intelligence. The acuteness with which Maggie's sensations are rendered and the ironic sympathy which plays over Maggie's relatives, so that the reader sees them both as the child saw them and as the mature artist comprehends them, is comparable to Proust's recreation of his childhood world in *Du Coté de chez Swann*. It is partly because Maggie's childhood and adolescence are so fully treated that the closing episodes appear melodramatic and unconvincing; it was also George Eliot's own view that the close of her novel suffered because she had treated the first part too fully to allow herself the necessary space to prepare the tragic climax. This view does not, however, offer a complete explanation of what goes wrong. After agreeing with Sir Edward Bulwer Lytton's criticism of the composition, she added, in her letter to Blackwood:

The other chief point of criticism—Maggie's position towards Stephen—is too vital a part of my whole conception and purpose for me to be converted to the condemnation of it. If I am wrong there—if I did not really know what my heroine would do under the circumstances in which I deliberately placed her—I ought not to have written this book at all, but quite a different book, if any. If the ethics of art do not admit the truthful presentation of a character essentially noble, but liable to great error—error that is anguish to its own nobleness—then, it seems to me, the ethics of art are too narrow, and must be widened to correspond with a widening psychology.[1]

We cannot know the precise form of the criticism she was here dealing with. But the last sentence raises a side-issue about which the modern reader of *The Mill on the Floss* is not really concerned, even if the Victorian reader was.[2] In former times art had constantly treated the 'character essentially noble, but liable to great error'. The words are almost a paraphrase of Aristotle's definition of the tragic hero, and the typical hero of great tragedy from Oedipus to Othello has constantly conformed to it. It is true that it is a conception that rarely occurs in English prose fiction before George Eliot. She was more aware than her immediate predecessors of the complexity of character and her creations cannot be labelled good or bad, nor accorded the wholesale approval or disapproval of the reader as readily as can many Victorian heroes or heroines. But the question at issue for the modern reader is not whether so 'noble' a character as Maggie could be mastered by passion, even if it is, in part, whether Stephen Guest is presented as an adequate temptation. Some defect in the drawing of Stephen is a contributory cause of dissatisfaction with the end of the book, and this defect is a probable result of the relative brevity with which this part of the

[1] Cross, vol. II, p. 262.
[2] Ruskin, in *Fiction, Fair and Foul*, wrote 'All healthy and helpful literature sets simple bars between right and wrong...while in the railway novel, interest is obtained with the vulgar reader for the vilest character, because the author describes carefully to his recognition the blotches, burrs and pimples in which the paltry nature resembles his own.... *The Mill on the Floss* is perhaps the most striking instance extant of this study of cutaneous disease. There is not a single person in the book of the smallest importance to anybody in the world, but themselves, whose qualities deserve so much as a line of printer's type in their description. There is no girl alive, fairly clever, half-educated, and unluckily related, whose life has not at least as much in it as Maggie's, to be described and to be pitied. Tom is a clumsy and cruel lout with the making of better things in him...while the rest of the characters are simply the sweepings out of a Pentonville omnibus.'

composition is treated. The other main characters concerned in the tragedy have been lived with throughout the novel: Tom and Lucy, Philip Wakem and Maggie herself have been known to the reader since their childhood. An intimate understanding of their nature and their development has been established in the first part of the novel. But Stephen Guest, although much of his childhood must have been spent at St Ogg's, was in a sufficiently different social world for his path not to have crossed with theirs. We meet him first as Lucy's accepted suitor (though it is an essential part of George Eliot's idea of her subject that there is no recognized engagement between them). Stephen makes an initially disagreeable impression on the reader:

... the fine young man who is leaning down from his chair to snap the scissors in the extremely abbreviated face of the 'King Charles' lying on the young lady's feet, is no other than Mr Stephen Guest, whose diamond ring, attar of roses, and air of nonchalant leisure, at twelve o'clock in the day, are the graceful and odoriferous result of the largest oil-mill and the most extensive wharf in St Ogg's.[1]

There is every reason to suppose that George Eliot intends the impression to be disagreeable, he is a vulgarian, compared with Arthur Donnithorne, a coxcomb and an insensitive egotist compared with Philip Wakem, a man without chivalry and without perception compared with Bob Jakin, a man without conscience or principle compared with Adam Bede. As all these impressions are the direct result of George Eliot's own creative activity, it is unlikely, on the face of it, that they occur against her will. She meant to show the development of better things in Stephen's nature under the influence of his love for Maggie. (There is a parallel in the treatment of Lydgate in *Middlemarch*, but, partly owing to greater artistic maturity and partly to the fuller time allowed for the required development, the intention is there successfully carried out.) Stephen, at this first appearance, imagines himself in love with Lucy and likes to 'smile down from his tall height, with the air of a rather patronising lover, at the little lady on the music stool'. Consciousness of his own

[1] *The Mill on the Floss*, bk. vi, ch. .

superiority is an important element in the pleasure he takes in 'that stage of courtship which makes the most exquisite moment of youth—where each is sure of the other's love, but no formal declaration has been made'. The character of Stephen emerges in this chapter largely by means of dialogue, and George Eliot had a fine ear for characteristic speech; but her method allows also of an explicit account of the motives for Stephen's choice of Lucy, in the last paragraph of this chapter she asks, with unmistakably ironic intention at Stephen's expense:

Was not Stephen Guest right in his decided opinion that this slim maiden of eighteen was quite the sort of wife a man would not be likely to repent of marrying?—a woman who was loving and thoughtful for other women, not giving them Judas-kisses with eyes askance on their welcome defects, but with real care and vision for their half-hidden pains and mortifications, with long ruminating enjoyment of little pleasures prepared for them? Perhaps the emphasis of his admiration did not fall precisely on this rarest quality in her—perhaps he approved his own choice of her chiefly because she did not strike him as a remarkable rarity. A man likes his wife to be pretty...but not to a maddening extent. A man likes his wife to be accomplished, gentle, affectionate, and not stupid; and Lucy had all these qualifications. Stephen was not surprised to find himself in love with her, and was conscious of excellent judgment in preferring her to Miss Leyburn, the daughter of the county member, although Lucy was only the daughter of his father's subordinate partner; besides, he had had to defy and overcome a slight unwillingness and disappointment in his father and sisters—a circumstance which gives a young man an agreeable consciousness of his own dignity. Stephen was aware that he had sense and independence enough to choose the wife who was likely to make him happy, unbiassed by any indirect considerations. He meant to choose Lucy: she was a little darling, and exactly the sort of woman he had always most admired.[1]

The whole point of this paragraph is to underline the self-regarding motives of Stephen's choice. 'The emphasis of his admiration' and his self-approval of his choice missed what was really excellent in Lucy, it was essential for George Eliot's

[1] *The Mill on the Floss*, bk. VI, ch. I.

purpose that Lucy's excellence should be clearly established, but Stephen chose her in blindness to her real virtues. He chose her very deliberately and approved of himself for doing so: she was 'exactly the sort of woman he most admired', much as Harriet Smith was, for Emma Woodhouse, 'exactly the something her home required'.

In the next chapter Stephen meets Maggie, who is in many ways the opposite of this sort of woman; she is markedly intelligent, instead of merely 'not stupid'. She is tall, dark, striking looking, instead of small, fair and pretty. She is angular and unconventional, instead of pliant and conformist. The author's intention is that, in total contrast to his deliberate choosing of Lucy, he shall be mastered by passionate love for a woman he would never have thought of choosing, and that the experience shall shatter his complacency, humble his masculine vanity and give a new depth to his character which will become capable of tragic suffering. There is not space enough for her to convince us of this development of Stephen's character, nor does she achieve for the reader sufficient intimacy with him to establish compassionate understanding. Her heroine concerns her far more. Nor would her partial failure with Stephen matter so much if she were wholly successful with Maggie in this part of the book. But the two are interdependent. It is essential that the reader should be able to feel with Maggie when her love for Philip Wakem is overwhelmed by a stronger feeling, unlike any she has hitherto experienced. The relation with Philip has been gradually unfolded in the first part of the novel. Philip has won Maggie's love both because, as a cripple, he commands her pity and because his keen and well-furnished mind wins her respect. But the passionate, sensual element has never entered into her feeling for him. The combination of attractions by which she is bound to him resemble those that draw Dorothea to Casaubon in *Middlemarch*; it is obvious in both novels that George Eliot has a complete understanding of this type of experience and that her art can communicate it fully. But to communicate the experience of 'falling in love' when that experience includes the inexplicable delight given by the physical presence, the voice, gestures, mannerisms of the beloved, is far more difficult. Probably the less the artist attempts to convey those physical characteristics in detail to the reader the better. Certainly the mannerisms of Ladislaw in *Middlemarch* often produce an opposite effect on the reader from that which they are intended to produce: they seem calculated to irritate rather than to delight. Most mannerisms do, except when seen with the eyes of love. Stephen Guest is far from being physically charming to the reader of *The Mill on the Floss*. There is an artistic failure to carry the reader along with Maggie at this point. We understand what happens to her, but we do not feel with her. And this is an element in the dissatisfaction we feel with this part of the work; but it does not explain the whole of it. An important part of it is due to the invention and treatment of the moral problem which is to be the climax of the story.

George Eliot's conception of moral choice required that her heroine should be faced with a dilemma out of which there was no happy issue. She was to be forced to choose between two alternatives, either of which would cause suffering, and the decision she reached was to depend upon her own prevision of the effect of her choice upon the other people involved in it. Her motive would be to cause as little unhappiness as the circumstances would allow and this would involve her in the difficulty that, George Eliot believed, is in the nature of such choices. The difference between right and wrong was not to be clear-cut, no preconceived principles should determine what the heroine had to do. That must depend upon Maggie's own perception of all the circumstances relevant to her act. In the early part of the book George Eliot had drawn freely on her own self-knowledge and memories in creating Maggie. Consequently, the invention of a suitable moral dilemma was perplexed by her own private life. She would obviously avoid any situation too closely resembling her own when she elected to live with Lewes. A part of what is wrong with the close of the novel is that the problem facing Maggie and Stephen at the crisis is not a satisfactory vehicle for the conception the author intended to symbolize by it. It is relevant to recall, in connection with Maggie's problem, George Eliot's dissatisfaction with Charlotte Brontë's treatment of Jane Eyre's problem, a dissatisfaction which most modern readers share in some degree. It cannot (even apart from the altered legal position) seem self-evident to us as it did to Charlotte Brontë that the decision Jane arrives at is right and that its contrary would have been wrong. On the other hand, Charlotte Brontë treats her climax with complete assurance; and, though there are manifest imperfections in the novel, the chapter in which Jane resists Rochester's persuasions is an admirable artistic success. Everything that is said in it by either lover carries complete conviction. Jane makes her choice by a courageous and obstinate adherence to a preconceived principle. At one moment she glances at the motive of worldly wisdom and self-protection. Rochester has told her of former mistresses of whom he grew weary:

I felt the truth of these words; and I drew from them the certain inference, that if I were so far to forget myself and all the teaching that had ever been instilled into me, as—under any pretext—with any justification—through any temptation—to become the successor of these poor girls, he would one day regard me with the same feeling which now in his mind desecrated their memory.[1]

But, as the scene progresses, it becomes as obvious to Jane as to the reader that Rochester's love for her is of a different kind from anything he ever felt for those others, or that they ever deserved that he should feel. When she says, 'You will forget me before I forget you', she is convinced by his answer:

'You make me a liar by such language: you sully my honour. I declared I could not change: you tell me to my face that I shall change soon. And what a distortion in your judgment, what a perversity in your ideas, is proved by your conduct! Is it better to drive a fellow-creature to despair than to transgress a mere human law—no man being injured by the breach? for you have neither near relatives nor acquaintances whom you need fear to offend by living with me.'

[1] Charlotte Brontë, *Jane Eyre*, ch. XXVII.

This was true: and while he spoke my very conscience and reason turned traitors against me, and charged me with crime in resisting him. They spoke almost as loud as Feeling: and that clamoured wildly. 'Oh, comply!' it said. 'Think of his misery; think of his danger—look at his state when left alone; remember his headlong nature; consider the recklessness following on despair—soothe him; save him; love him; tell him you love him and will be his. Who in the world cares for *you*? or who will be injured by what you do?'

Still indomitable was the reply—'*I* care for myself. The more solitary, the more friendless, the more unsustained I am, the more I will respect myself. I will keep the law given by God; sanctioned by man. I will hold to the principles received by me when I was sane, and not mad—as I am now. Laws and principles are not for the times when there is no temptation: they are for such moments as this, when body and soul rise in mutiny against their vigour; stringent are they; inviolate they shall be. If at my individual convenience I might break them, what would be their worth? They have a worth—so I have always believed; and if I cannot believe it now, it is because I am insane—quite insane: with my veins running fire and my heart beating faster than I can count its throbs. Preconceived opinions, foregone determinations, are all I have at this hour to stand by me: there I plant my foot.'[1]

Charlotte Brontë can afford to give Rochester all the cards: his love is genuine; it is affection and admiration conjoint with passion; there is every probability that it will endure. There is no one connected either with him or with Jane who can be injured by their union. She can afford to give Jane every rational motive for surrender, because, according to her code, surrender would be a sin in itself; it is wrong to live with a man who is legally and religiously bound to another woman. It is right to refuse to do so whatever the consequences may be. For Charlotte Brontë the rule of right is absolute. The question 'Who will be injured by what you do?' is irrelevant; but for George Eliot it is all-important:

The sanctions of religion were indifferent to her after rejecting its doctrines and also, granted sufficient cause, she was prepared to disregard the social law of England.[2]

---

[1] *Jane Eyre*, ch. XXVII.   [2] Acton, *Historical Essays & Studies.*

Lord Acton wrote this in explanation of the decision George Eliot herself made to live with George Henry Lewes as his wife. It is a just description of her conception of moral problems. They must be solved as they arise, with due consideration of every circumstance; the right solution will depend upon the consequences of the choice when it is made and there is no absolute code that can serve instead of an attempt to foresee those consequences.

Maggie is mastered by the first onrush of her passionate love for Stephen which springs to meet his love for her. She allows the bond between them to tighten, by imperceptible degrees, into an almost unbreakable tie. Possibly the limitation of space does not allow George Eliot scope enough to convince us of the insidious and gradual development of the feeling, but her conception is clearly discoverable. Maggie advances by definite stages from a private recognition of her own state of feeling to an avowal of it to Stephen and both are fully conscious of their danger when she agrees to go alone with him on the boating expedition. Lucy had withdrawn from the party herself, believing that Stephen was not going and that Philip and Maggie would be alone together. She had discerned some understanding between them and hoped to further it. Maggie herself looked forward to being alone with Philip:

> She was almost glad of the plan; for perhaps it would bring her some strength and calmness to be alone with Philip again.

But Philip, fevered with anxiety about Stephen and Maggie, whose mutual attraction he also is aware of, is too ill to come. Stephen arrives alone. For a few moments Maggie resists the temptation, but it does not seem a very serious one and she soon yields.

Stephen is all along more conscious of what he is doing; he is allowing the circumstances to lead on to the fulfilment of his desires, even if he is not actually contriving them. But it is with Maggie's conscience that the author is concerned. Stephen rows past the stopping-place at Luckreth half aware of what he is doing while Maggie is wholly unaware. But she has allowed her 'natural impulse' to take charge, and the moral sanctions accepted by George Eliot exact, as sternly as the traditional standards, that natural impulses be controlled by reasoned judgement. The description of the boat gliding through the waters symbolizes the way Maggie is letting things slide:

They glided rapidly along, Stephen rowing, helped by the backward-flowing tide, past the Tofton trees and houses—on between the silent sunny fields and pastures, which seemed filled with a natural joy that had no reproach for theirs. The breath of the young, unwearied day, the delicious rhythmic dip of the oars, the fragmentary song of a passing bird heard now and then, as if it were only the overflowing of brim-full gladness, the sweet solitude of a twofold consciousness that was mingled into one by that grave untiring gaze which need not be averted—what else could there be in their minds for the first hour? Some low, subdued, languid exclamation of love came from Stephen from time to time, as he went on rowing idly, half automatically: otherwise, they spoke no word; for what could words have been but an inlet to thought? and thought did not belong to that enchanted haze in which they were enveloped—it belonged to the past and the future that lay outside the haze. Maggie was only dimly conscious of the banks, as they passed them, and dwelt with no recognition on the villages: she knew there were several to be passed before they reached Luckreth, where they always stopped and left the boat. At all times she was so liable to fits of absence, that she was likely enough to let her way-marks pass unnoticed.

But at last Stephen, who had been rowing more and more idly, ceased to row, laid down the oars, folded his arms, and looked down on the water as if watching the pace at which the boat glided without his help. This sudden change roused Maggie. She looked at the far-stretching fields—at the banks close by—and felt that they were entirely strange to her. A terrible alarm took possession of her.[1]

By this time it is too late to choose her way. To get back to St Ogg's that night is impossible and whatever decision Maggie makes on the following morning she cannot avert the suffering that her yielding has caused. This fact alters the character of the moral conflict that follows and even confuses the issues. The

[1] *The Mill on the Floss*, bk. VI, ch. XIII.

conflict itself is as moving and convincing a dramatic scene as that between Jane Eyre and Rochester and, like that, is given almost entirely through the thoughts and speech of the characters. Maggie's feelings, like Jane's, are consistent with all that we know of her past experience and of her temperament.

But when Stephen wakes and the conflict of wills takes place between the two the issues are not clear-cut as they are between Jane and Rochester. There are no fixed principles involved, dependent on the laws of revealed religion or of the society to which they both belong, and the principle Maggie tries to discover, which depends on the consequences of an act, eludes her because so many consequences are already determined. The passionate argument between the two moves in circles; it cannot advance and grow clearer because Maggie's decision is the result of feeling and not of thought. When Stephen first addresses her in the morning he assumes that she will accept the situation:

'Here we are in sight of Mudport', he said, at last. 'Now, dearest', he added, turning towards her with a look that was half-beseeching, 'the worst part of your fatigue is over. On the land we can command swiftness. In another hour and a half we shall be in a chaise together—and that will seem rest to you after this.'

Maggie felt it was time to speak: it would only be unkind now to assent by silence. She spoke in the lowest tone, as he had done, but with distinct decision.

'We shall not be together—we shall have parted.'

The blood rushed to Stephen's face.

'We shall not', he said. 'I'll die first.'

It was as she had dreaded—there was a struggle coming. But neither of them dared to say another word, till the boat was let down, and they were taken to the landing-place. Here there was a cluster of gazers and passengers awaiting the departure of the steamboat to St Ogg's. Maggie had a dim sense, when she had landed, and Stephen was hurrying her along on his arm, that some one had advanced towards her from that cluster as if he were coming to speak to her. But she was hurried along, and was indifferent to everything but the coming trial.

A porter guided them to the nearest inn and posting-house, and Stephen gave the order for the chaise as they passed through the yard.

Maggie took no notice of this, and only said, 'Ask them to show us into a room where we can sit down.'

When they entered, Maggie did not sit down, and Stephen, whose face had a desperate determination in it, was about to ring the bell, when she said, in a firm voice—

'I'm not going: we must part here.'

'Maggie', he said, turning round towards her, and speaking in the tones of a man who feels a process of torture beginning, 'do you mean to kill me? What is the use of it now? The whole thing is done.'

'No, it is not done', said Maggie. 'Too much is done—more than we can ever remove the trace of. But I will go no farther. Don't try to prevail with me again. I couldn't choose yesterday.'[1]

And at the end of the argument each is saying the same things as each said at first:

'Dearest', he said, in his deepest, tenderest tone, leaning towards her, and putting his arm round her, 'you *are* mine now—the world believes it—duty must spring out of that now: in a few hours you will be legally mine, and those who had claims on us will submit—they will see that there was a force which declared against their claims.'

Maggie's eyes opened wide in one terrified look at the face that was close to hers, and she started up—pale again.

'Oh, I can't do it', she said, in a voice almost of agony—'Stephen—don't ask me—don't urge me. I can't argue any longer—I don't know what is wise; but my heart will not let me do it. I see—I feel their trouble now: it is as if it were branded on my mind. *I* have suffered, and had no one to pity me; and now I have made others suffer. It would never leave me; it would embitter your love for me. I *do* care for Philip—in a different way: I remember all we said to each other; I know how he thought of me as the one promise of his life. He was given to me that I might make his lot less hard; and I have forsaken him. And Lucy—she has been deceived—she who trusted me more than any one. I cannot marry you: I cannot take a good for myself that has been wrung out of their misery. It is not the force that ought to rule us—this that we feel for each other; it would rend me away from all that my past life has made dear and holy to me. I can't set out on a fresh life, and forget that: I must go back to it, and cling to it, else I shall feel as if there were nothing firm beneath my feet.'

[1] *The Mill on the Floss*, bk. VI, ch. XIV.

'Good God, Maggie', said Stephen, rising too and grasping her arm, 'you rave. How can you go back without marrying me? You don't know what will be said, dearest. You see nothing as it really is.'

'Yes, I do. But they will believe me. I will confess everything. Lucy will believe me—she will forgive you, and,—and—oh, *some* good will come by clinging to the right. Dear, dear Stephen, let me go!—don't drag me into deeper remorse. My whole soul has never consented—it does not consent now.'

Maggie can refuse to go forward to marriage with Stephen and the enjoyment of a selfish happiness; but she cannot go back and save Lucy and Philip from the misery of knowing that they are not loved. Ultimately they may think better of her because of this sacrifice she is making, but for themselves it cannot bring happiness nor much alleviate pain. It is therefore hard for the reader to believe that this sacrifice of her own and Stephen's happiness is worth while. More important is the fact that the real error does not seem to be the one of which Maggie is conscious. When we apply the moral standards that the author herself invites us to apply we feel that Maggie and Stephen should have shown more courage and honesty when they first discovered that they were in love. Their intention to marry Philip and Lucy in spite of that discovery seems the reverse of noble. That intended deception shocks the reader more than does the failure to carry it out. The qualities needed in their difficult situation were not self-sacrificing heroism, but patience and tact and delicacy of feeling. They needed to allow time to pass so that they might test the durability of their love for each other and, if it stood the test, extricate themselves from their former ties without needless cruelty. But one must not, at this point, identify Maggie and her view of her situation, with George Eliot herself. One difference between Jane Eyre's moral conflict and Maggie's is that in the former the identity of outlook between author and heroine is complete and in the latter it is not. When, after Maggie's return to St Ogg's, she seeks the advice of Dr Kenn, George Eliot uses this character to express her own views, and this employment of a wise, disinterested spectator as a commentator on the action and, as it were, a lens through which the reader may see it in a new perspective, is comparable to the similar device used later by Henry James or Joseph Conrad. But this method is, in *The Mill on the Floss*, embryonic only. Dr Kenn's reflections indicate the complexity of George Eliot's conception; but they are too undeveloped to communicate it fully.

When Maggie had left him, Dr Kenn stood ruminating with his hands behind him, and his eyes fixed on the carpet, under a painful sense of doubt and difficulty. The tone of Stephen's letter, which he had read, and the actual relations of all the persons concerned, forced upon him powerfully the idea of an ultimate marriage between Stephen and Maggie as the least evil; and the impossibility of their proximity in St Ogg's on any other supposition, until after years of separation, threw an insurmountable prospective difficulty over Maggie's stay there. On the other hand, he entered with all the comprehension of a man who had known spiritual conflict, and lived through years of devoted service to his fellow-men, into that state of Maggie's heart and conscience which made the consent to the marriage a desecration to her: her conscience must not be tampered with: the principle on which she had acted was a safer guide than any balancing of consequences. His experience told him that intervention was too dubious a responsibility to be lightly incurred: the possible issue either of an endeavour to restore the former relations with Lucy and Philip, or of counselling submission to this irruption of a new feeling, was hidden in a darkness all the more impenetrable because each immediate step was clogged with evil.

The great problem of the shifting relation between passion and duty is clear to no man who is capable of apprehending it: the question whether the moment has come in which a man has fallen below the possibility of a renunciation that will carry any efficacy, and must accept the sway of a passion against which he had struggled as a trespass, is one for which we have no master-key that will fit all cases. The casuists have become a byword of reproach; but their perverted spirit of minute discrimination was the shadow of a truth to which eyes and hearts are too often fatally sealed—the truth, that moral judgments must remain false and hollow, unless they are checked and enlightened by a perpetual reference to the special circumstances that mark the individual lot.[1]

[1] *The Mill on the Floss*, bk. VII, ch. II.

Clearly Maggie, in her youth and inexperience, is only fumbling after the conception that the author here enunciates in her own person and through the mind of Dr Kenn. Maggie can only rely on the moral sense, or conscience that her temperament, her upbringing and her environment have combined to develop in her. But the total effect that George Eliot seems to be trying to produce is more complex than she can achieve in the form of fiction she is using. To express her own consciousness of the subtle discriminations necessary to the just solution of a moral problem, and to set against this the gropings of a girl who has little to rely on except her instincts, required more space and a different artistic form. Henry James was to treat situations of a comparable kind in long novels wholly devoted to their unravelling (*The Wings of a Dove*, *The Ambassadors* and *The Golden Bowl*). George Eliot is hampered by the traditional form and also by current moral assumptions. The former leads her to attempt too much in the last sixth of a work already overflowing with varied interests. The latter, presumably, accounts for her missing the cruelty that underlies the seemingly virtuous intention of Maggie and Stephen to dissemble their love and carry out their undeclared engagements. She had carefully arranged that they should be bound by no legal tie—not even by an engagement, which her Victorian readers would have thought almost as binding (compare Trollope's *Can You Forgive Her?*). Their decision was to depend on the rational conception of virtue—the weighing of foreseeable consequences. But, in fact, Maggie falls back on the assumption that 'all self-sacrifice is good'. Before she burnt Stephen's last pleading letter:

She sat quite still, far on into the night: with no impulse to change her attitude, without active force enough even for the mental act of prayer: only waiting for the light that would surely come again. It came with the memories that no passion could long quench: the long past came back to her, and with it the fountains of self-renouncing pity and affection, of faithfulness and resolve. The words that were marked by the quiet hand in the little old book that she had long ago learned by heart, rushed even to her lips, and found a vent for themselves in a low murmur that was quite lost in the loud driving of the rain against the window and the loud moan and roar of the wind: 'I have received the Cross, I have received it from Thy hand; I will bear it, and bear it till death, as Thou hast laid it upon me.'[1]

After she has burnt the letter she has nothing left to hope for except an early death and the author provides the timely, wish-fulfilling death by drowning. It is emotionally satisfying that Maggie should attempt to save Tom's life, that the brother and sister should die in each other's arms, and that Tom's eyes should at last be opened to his sister's worth:

...a new revelation to his spirit, of the depths in life, that had lain beyond his vision which he had fancied so keen and clear.[2]

But when we reflect we cannot but feel that this poetic justice at the culminating point of a long, serious, naturalistic novel, is a dishonest contrivance. George Eliot has cut the knot she was unable to unravel. She has placed Maggie in a dilemma in which no preconceived principle could direct her choice—she has let her choose and then she has refused to imagine the results of her choice. We are temporarily carried away by the vivid description of her death, but the inflated, melodramatic style of the close is a symptom of the relaxation of the author's serious concern with her characters.

The Mill on the Floss is among the major English novels, but it holds that position in spite of grave defects. It owes it to the invention and the masterly presentation of the Tulliver family and the Dodson aunts, to the story of Maggie's childhood and adolescence in the world they inhabit, and to the humour and compassion with which the author conceives and presents that world. But the imperfect fraction of the novel, Book VI, has within it the seed of a new development in English fiction which will ultimately come to rich fruition in the works of Conrad and Henry James and which was to prosper better in some of George Eliot's later work than it did in her second novel.

[1] *The Mill on the Floss*, bk. VII, ch. v.   [2] Ibid.

CHAPTER VII

SILAS MARNER

THE first period of George Eliot's creative activity ends with *Silas Marner*, conceived and completed between the end of November 1860 and March 1861. The story of *The Weaver of Raveloe* is a poetic conception and it was in this light that George Eliot herself thought of her story of a man, simple and trusting by nature, who, by the deliberate act of a false friend, is accused and convicted of theft. He is sundered from the community in which he was rooted and deprived at one blow of his faith in man and God—for his guilt had been 'proved' by the simple method of drawing lots and he and his co-religionists believed that the divine hand would point out the sinner. Isolated from his kind, he goes to live among strangers, and gives his heart to the lonely accumulation of gold. Then he is drawn back into the health-giving life of the community by a child. In February 1861 George Eliot wrote to Blackwood, who had been reading the first chapters:

I don't wonder at your finding my story, as far as you have read it, rather sombre: indeed, I should not have believed that any one would have been interested in it but myself (since Wordsworth is dead) if Mr Lewes had not been strongly arrested by it. But I hope you will not find it at all a sad story, as a whole, since it sets—or is intended to set—in a strong light the remedial influences of pure, natural human relations. The Nemesis is a very mild one. I have felt all through as if the story would have lent itself best to metrical rather than to prose fiction, especially in all that relates to the psychology of Silas; except that, under that treatment, there could not be an equal play of humour. It came to me first of all quite suddenly, as a sort of legendary tale, suggested by my recollection of having once, in early childhood, seen a linen weaver with a bag on his back; but as my mind dwelt on the subject, I became inclined to a more realistic treatment.[1]

[1] Cross, vol. II, p. 290.

It is fortunate that George Eliot decided to write her story in prose. She was incomparably more gifted as a prose than as a verse writer; her blank verse works of fiction are conscientious, competent and dull. In them the preconceived moral idea is always obtrusive because, when she composes in verse, she is never swept onward by the flow of creative energy. Moreover, as is evident in what she here writes to Blackwood, she shared the widespread mid-nineteenth-century view that 'metrical composition' implied a peculiar solemnity.[1]

According to her own account, if she had written the book in verse, she would have felt bound to exclude the 'play of humour', which is an important factor in its success. Another is the freshness and apparently effortless freedom of its style which is partly due to her confidence in the story as adequate to convey its own moral, so that didactic asides hardly occur, and partly to the spontaneity and speed of composition which would almost certainly have been slowed down if she had chosen verse as her medium. Nothing was lost by writing in prose provided the reader has no inhibiting preconceptions about the nature of prose narrative. He must be ready to accept improbable events as readily as he would accept them in a poem, for the story is undoubtedly improbable. But once the framework of the plot is accepted the truth to life, within that framework, is convincing. We must willingly suspend disbelief when we discover that the first Mrs Godfrey Cass, having poisoned herself with drugs, has died at a convenient spot, after walking some miles through the snow, carrying a child old enough to toddle. She must have been unusually strong, for a child of that size is not easy to carry; but that is to consider too closely. We must believe—and the author beguiles us into belief if we will allow her—that the golden-haired baby leaves the dead mother at a point just near enough to Silas's cottage for it to totter into it and so be found, a living substitute for the lost golden hoard. Further, we must accept the

---

[1] Much misunderstanding of such poems as Wordsworth's *The Idiot Boy* is still the result of supposing that a serious poem must be solemn and that the poet cannot have intended the reader to be amused.

SILAS MARNER

coincidence that Dunsey Cass falls into the stone pit near-by, and that his corpse and Silas's stolen treasure are not discovered until sixteen years later, on the eve of Eppie's marriage. Nor must we question the likelihood that Nancy's baby daughter died in infancy and that Nancy and Godfrey could never have another child. None of these things is in itself impossible. The reliance on coincidence to bring about the redemption of Silas and the 'mild' Nemesis for Godfrey is much less than the reliance Hardy often puts on it to translate his more pessimistic vision. Once these events are accepted the conduct of the story carries conviction; Silas, Eppie and Godfrey behave with entire consistency and develop in accordance with their nature.

George Eliot's fertility of invention and assurance in the creation of character is the more remarkable in *Silas Marner*, since her choice of the place and time for her story excludes any character whose intellectual and moral experience resembles her own. In the provincial town of St Ogg's in the early nineteenth century, and in families wealthy enough to seek the private tuition of the clergy for their children, she could provide Maggie with a few crumbs of knowledge to whet her appetite for more. Maggie's unsatisfied intelligence is a part of the theme of *The Mill on the Floss*. But, in Raveloe, 'in the days when the spinning-wheels hummed busily in the farmhouses', no one suffers from intellectual hunger. George Eliot has here escaped from her own world of intellectual curiosity, as well as from the life of the city, which she was finding oppressive. On 28 November 1860, she wrote in her journal:

> Since I last wrote in this Journal, I have suffered much from physical weakness, accompanied with mental depression. The loss of the country has seemed very bitter to me, and my want of health and strength has prevented me from working much—still worse, has made me despair of ever working well again....I am engaged now in writing a story—the idea of which came to me after our arrival in this house, and which has thrust itself between me and the other book I was meditating.

Her rustic tale served her, among other things, as a means of rediscovering the rural world for which she was homesick and

133

in which she could focus her attention on the Wordsworthian 'primary pains and pleasures' of simple people.

The community of Raveloe is confined, spiritually and intellectually, within the narrow bounds of early nineteenth-century village life. The Christian observances, baptism, Sabbath-keeping and occasional communion are accepted within the community as semi-magical rites or as pious customs.

> The inhabitants of Raveloe were not severely regular in their church-going, and perhaps there was hardly a person in the parish who would not have held that to go to church every Sunday in the calendar would have shown a greedy desire to stand well with Heaven, and get an undue advantage over their neighbours—a wish to be better than the 'common run' that would have implied a reflection on those who had had godfathers and godmothers as well as themselves, and had an equal right to the burying-service.[1]

There is so little curiosity about the fundamental Christian doctrines (as distinct from Christian ethics and Christian customs) that Dolly Winthrop cannot discover anything in common between her religion and the Methodism in which Silas had been brought up. When, after the loss of his money, she goes to try and comfort him she suggests that he would be happier if he went to church with his neighbours at any rate

> ...'upo' Christmas-day, this blessed Christmas as is ever coming',

and Silas answers:

> 'Nay, nay, I know nothing o' church. I've never been to church.'
> 'No!' said Dolly, in a low tone of wonderment. Then bethinking herself of Silas's advent from an unknown country, she said, 'Could it ha' been as they'd no church where you was born?'
> 'Oh yes', said Silas, meditatively, sitting in his usual posture of leaning on his knees, and supporting his head. 'There was churches—a many—it was a big town. But I knew nothing of 'em—I went to chapel.'

[1] *Silas Marner*, ch. x.

Dolly was much puzzled at this new word, but she was rather afraid of inquiring further, lest 'chapel' might mean some haunt of wickedness. After a little thought she said—

'Well, Master Marner, it's niver too late to turn over a new leaf, and if you've niver had no church, there's no telling the good it'll do you. For I feel so set up and comfortable as niver was when I've been and heard the prayers, and the singing to the praise and glory o' God, as Mr Macey gives out; and Mr Crackenthorp saying good words, and more partic'lar on Sacramen' Day. And if a bit o' trouble comes, I feel as I can put up wi' it, for I've looked for help i' the right quarter, and gev myself up to Them as we must all give ourselves up to at the last; and if we'n done our part, it isn't to be believed as Them as are above us 'ull be worse nor we are, and come short o' Their'n.'

Poor Dolly's exposition of her simple Raveloe theology fell rather unmeaningly on Silas's ears, for there was no word in it that could rouse a memory of what he had known as religion, and his comprehension was quite baffled by the plural pronoun, which was no heresy of Dolly's, but only her way of avoiding a presumptuous familiarity.

The squirearchy of Raveloe are hardly more sophisticated than the rustics; their mental world is almost as remote from that of their author. But they belong to a realm of thought and feeling that surrounded her as a child and from which her most untrammelled creative power springs. The peculiar quality of the whole book arises from the limitations of the field which excludes all the metaphysical problems with which her mind had been long occupied. The characters, with the exception of the two evildoers Dunsey Cass and the first Mrs Godfrey Cass—who, when they have set the plot in motion disappear—are all drawn with an easy assurance and persuasive truth to life. They speak in an idiom which is characteristic of a class and a time, but which also sharply defines the individual character. This is as evident with a minor character, such as Priscilla Lammeter as it is with her sister Nancy:

'It drives me past patience', said Priscilla, impetuously, 'that way o' the men—always wanting and wanting, and never easy with what they've got. They can't sit comfortable in their chairs when they've neither ache nor pain, but either they must stick a pipe in their mouths, to make 'em better than well, or else they must be swallowing something strong, though they're forced to make haste before the next meal comes in. But joyful be it spoken, our father was never that sort o' man. And if it had pleased God to make you ugly like me, so as the men wouldn't ha' run after you, we might have kept to our own family, and had nothing to do with folks as have got uneasy blood in their veins.'[1]

The tactless, forthright speech is as idiosyncratic as is Nancy's reply in swift defence of her husband.

George Eliot's insight into Nancy's character is unfaltering and never more so than when she allows her to behave in a way that neither the reader nor Nancy's own husband can foresee, when Eppie's real parentage is first revealed to her. Nancy's instinctive moral certitudes and her narrowness of judgement are counterbalanced by a warmth of heart and quickness of sympathy and the two aspects of her nature combine at this juncture to produce the response Godfrey least expects. She had resisted his plea to adopt Eppie when she did not know that Eppie was his child, because adoption conflicted with one of her 'rigid principles'.

To adopt a child because children of your own had been denied you was to try and choose your lot in spite of Providence....[2]

Her code, made up of custom and of precept, comprised absolutes to govern even small points of manners; before her marriage

she insisted on dressing like Priscilla, because 'it was right for sisters to dress alike', and because 'she would do what was right if she wore a gown dyed with cheese-colouring'.[3]

When the long-concealed past evil-doing comes to light, no wonder Godfrey expects this rigid naïve moralist to be unforgiving. Yet when she speaks there is no doubt that we hear the authentic accent of her character.

'Nancy', said Godfrey, slowly, 'when I married you, I hid something from you—something I ought to have told you. That woman Marner found dead in the snow—Eppie's mother—that wretched woman—was my wife: Eppie is my child.'

[1] *Silas Marner*, ch. XVII.   [2] Ibid.   [3] Ibid.

He paused, dreading the effect of his confession. But Nancy sat quite still, only that her eyes dropped and ceased to meet his. She was pale and quiet as a meditative statue, clasping her hands on her lap.

'You'll never think the same of me again', said Godfrey, after a little while, with some tremor in his voice.

She was silent.

'I oughtn't to have left the child unowned: I oughtn't to have kept it from you. But I couldn't bear to give you up, Nancy. I was led away into marrying her—I suffered for it.'

Still Nancy was silent, looking down; and he almost expected that she would presently get up and say she would go to her father's. How could she have any mercy for faults that must seem so black to her, with her simple severe notions?

But at last she lifted up her eyes to his again and spoke. There was no indignation in her voice—only deep regret.

'Godfrey, if you had but told me this six years ago, we could have done some of our duty by the child. Do you think I'd have refused to take her in, if I'd known she was yours?'[1]

Within the neatly articulated, simple, legendary plot of *Silas Marner* George Eliot creates a little world of sharply individualized characters. She presents them mainly by their own words and acts and her own commentary on their behaviour is never over-elaborate and never patronizing. She identifies herself with them and measures the compass of their ideas as securely as though she, herself, had never read any other book than the human heart. The furthest stretch of philosophical speculation in Raveloe is represented by the meditations of Mr Macey, tailor and parish clerk, with which he puzzles and entertains the company at the 'Rainbow' when they prompt him to tell again an old and favourite story about the wedding of the first Mr Lammeter:

'. . . Mr Drumlow—poor old gentleman, I was fond on him—but when he come to put the questions, he put 'em by the rule o' contrairy, like, and he says, "Wilt thou have this man to thy wedded wife?" says he; and then he says, "Wilt thou have this woman to thy wedded husband?" says he. But the partic'larest thing of all is, as nobody took any notice on it but me, and they answered straight off "Yes", like as if it had been

[1] *Silas Marner*, ch. XVIII.

me saying "Amen" i' the right place, without listening to what went before.'

'But *you* knew what was going on well enough, . . . You were live enough, eh?' said the butcher.

'Lor' bless you!' said Mr Macey, pausing, and smiling in pity at the impotence of his hearer's imagination—'why, I was all of a tremble: it was as if I'd been a coat pulled by the two tails, like; for I couldn't stop the parson, I couldn't take upon me to do that; and yet I said to myself, I says, "Suppose they shouldn't be fast married, 'cause the words are contrairy?" and my head went working like a mill, for I was allays uncommon for turning things over and seeing all round 'em; and I says to myself, "Is't the meanin' or the words as makes folks fast i' wedlock?" For the parson meant right, and the bride and bridegroom meant right. But then, when I come to think on it, meanin' goes but a little way i' most things, for you may mean to stick things together, and your glue may be bad, and then where are you? And so I says to mysen, "It isn't the meanin', it's the glue." And I was worreted as if I'd got three bells to pull at once, when we went into the vestry, and they begun to sign their names. But where's the use o' talking—you can't think what goes on in a 'cute man's inside.'[1]

This little novel that closes the first period is the most flawless of George Eliot's works. It is not the greatest since its small scale, its narrow world and its symbolical character precluded the exercise of some of her gifts. But nowhere else does her fiction carry all that she has to say so unobtrusively and effortlessly. It is natural that she should have thought of Wordsworth as the ideal audience for the story of the weaver whose soul withers away to a mere lust for gold when he is shut off from his kind by despair and then flowers again to full humanity when events draw him back within the community. And perhaps this is the only one of her books that was written throughout in the Wordsworthian mood of 'wise passiveness', and springs without conscious intellectual effort from 'emotion recollected in tranquillity'.

[1] *Silas Marner*, ch. VI.

CHAPTER VIII

ROMOLA

ON 28 August 1860, George Eliot wrote to John Blackwood:

> I think I must tell you the secret, though I am distrusting my powers
> to make it grow into a published fact. When we were in Florence, I was
> rather fired with the idea of writing a historical romance—scene,
> Florence; period, the close of the fifteenth century, which was marked
> by Savonarola's career and martyrdom. Mr Lewes has encouraged me
> to persevere in the project, saying that I should probably do something
> in historical romance rather different in character from what has been
> done before. But I want first to write another English story, and the
> plan I should like to carry out is this: to publish my next English novel
> when my Italian one is advanced enough for us to begin its publication
> a few months afterwards in 'Maga'. It would appear without a name
> in the Magazine, and be subsequently reprinted with the name of
> 'George Eliot'. I need not tell you the wherefore of this plan. You
> know well enough the received phrases with which a writer is greeted
> when he does something else than what is expected of him. But just
> now I am quite without confidence in my future doings, and almost
> repent of having formed conceptions which will go on lashing at me
> now until I have at least tried to fulfil them.[1]

Romola was the book she was meditating when *Silas Marner*
'thrust itself between' and this letter is the first account of the
project of writing the historical romance which was to cause her
so much agony of mind.

Throughout 1861 she was studying the background of her
subject in contemporary records and in histories of the period.
On 12 December 1861 her journal records:

> Finished writing my plot, of which I must make several other
> draughts before I begin to write my book.

[1] Cross, vol. II, p. 271.

And on 17 December 'studied the topography of Florence'.[1] On 1 January she underlines an entry: 'I began again my novel of "Romola".' Between January and July she had agreed to publish the novel in *The Cornhill Magazine*. 'There has been the regret of leaving Blackwood, who has written me a letter in the most perfect spirit of gentlemanliness and good feeling.'[2] She had refused the offer of George Smith of *The Cornhill Magazine* in March, because he wished to begin publishing in May and she could not then see her way clearly enough, 'and I cannot consent to begin publication until I have seen nearly to the end of the work'. Presumably by July she had the whole lay-out in mind, but the work was progressing slowly and painfully. On 10 July 'A dreadful palsy has beset me for the last few days. I have scarcely made any progress. Yet I have been very well in body.'[3] Publication in *The Cornhill Magazine* began in July 1862 and was complete by August 1863. She cannot have finished writing the book much before then since her journal for July 1863 records 'I am backward with my July number of *Romola*—the last part but one'. Her husband, J. W. Cross, writes:

I remember my wife telling me, at Witley, how cruelly she had suffered at Dorking from working under a leaden weight at this time. The writing of *Romola* ploughed into her more than any of her books. She told me she could put her finger on it as marking a well-defined transition in her life. In her own words, 'I began it a young woman,—I finished it an old woman'.[4]

Perhaps this almost unabating sense of effort accompanying the composition of *Romola* is not irrelevant to the fact that the book is, in comparison with *Adam Bede*, *The Mill on the Floss* or *Middlemarch*, a failure. It is a novel which could only have been the work of a gifted writer; it is the product of knowledge and wisdom and strenuous meditation: but something essential is missing; the interest flags and the illusion is not sustained. To read *Romola* is a fascinating exercise of the mind rather than an imaginative experience.

[1] Cross, vol. II, p. 324.   [2] Ibid., p. 339.
[3] Ibid., p. 340.   [4] Ibid., p. 352.

In all George Eliot's novels, with the exception of *Silas Marner*, it is possible to distinguish between an intellectual and an imaginative impulse. One can discern an element of thought that can be abstracted from the whole experience the fiction imparts; moral ideas that can be isolated and that were present in the author's mind before her story was conceived. She is a creative artist, but she is also a woman who had read and thought much, particularly about the nature of man and society, about the history of beliefs and about the relation between moral conduct and theological dogma. Her inquiry into theological questions had been prompted by a passionate concern for morality and, when she accepted the rationalist view that the supernatural is beyond the range of human knowledge, she sought all the more arduously for moral guidance within the natural world. Her search led her to the conclusion that the fruit of ill-doing is tasted in this life, both by the doer and by those on whom his personality and his deeds impinge. Her novels explore the way in which human character is formed by its own choices and then spreads its influence out in widening circles to those around. She believed in what she called 'meliorism' or the gradual improvement in man's lot which could not be effected by divine grace or any miraculous intervention, but only by the thoughts and deeds of men. These and other ideas—arising out of her reading, her discourse with friends and her conscious beliefs—contribute to her vision of life. But, though the quality of her novels is enhanced by her intelligence and her wisdom, no amount of wisdom and intelligence could, by themselves, make her a great novelist. The power to beguile the reader into an imagined world springs from the creative impulse, it is the faculty of imagination not of judgement that breathes life into the invented characters. The creative act requires some suspension of conscious intellectual effort, such as Keats describes in the phrase 'negative capability'. Proust, in *Du Coté de chez Swann* tells of how, as a boy, he despaired of becoming a writer, because he had no great philosophic ideas and then, quite unconnected, as he thought, with his abandoned literary ambitions, some visual impression or some scent or sound would insistently claim his attention, as though it held a secret within it. He usually resisted the contemplative effort that he knew would be necessary to discover that secret; but one day, because such an experience occurred when all the conditions were favourable to meditation, it bore fruit in a prose poem about the Church bells of Martinville. He had found himself powerless each time he sought for

...un sujet philosophique pour une grande œuvre littéraire,

and he did not at first recognize any relevance to his literary aspirations in experiences

...toujours liées à un objet particulier dépourvu de valeur intellectuelle et ne se rapportant à aucune vérité abstraite.

Yet these vivid sense impressions and the exercise of 'wise passiveness' in their contemplation, proved to be the source of his creative power. This is one instance, among many, in which a creative artist reveals that his impulse arises out of sense impressions, and flowers when conscious thought is in abeyance.[1] That impulse depended for George Eliot on her immediate impressions of people and places and it issued in the full understanding of a given person at a given moment and in the power to communicate a sense of the place, time and mental environment. It arose out of the perceptions of the ear and the eye, 'recollected in tranquillity'. One factor in the relative failure of *Romola* is that her aural and visual memories are of little service to her. She cannot, for instance, hear her Florentines speak. She relies on an intellectual reconstruction, as, for instance, when the barber Nello says:

'Good-day, Messer Domenico,...You come as opportunely as cheese on macaroni. Ah! you are in haste—wish to be shaved without delay—ecco! And this is a morning when every one has a grave matter on his mind. Florence orphaned—the very pivot of Italy snatched away—heaven itself at a loss what to do next. *Oimè!* Well, well; the sun is

[1] George Eliot herself gives an instance of this when she describes how she wrote the scene between Dorothea Brooke and Rosamond Vincy in *Middlemarch* (see p. 168).

nevertheless travelling on towards dinner-time again; and, as I was saying, you come like cheese ready grated. For this young stranger was wishing for an honourable trader who would advance him a sum on a certain ring of value, and if I had counted every goldsmith and money-lender in Florence on my fingers, I couldn't have found a better name than Menico Cennini. Besides, he hath other ware in which you deal,—Greek learning and young eyes,—a double implement which you printers are always in need of.'[1]

There is an obvious, conscious effort to find appropriate metaphors (such as cheese and macaroni) and to introduce a few Italian words (*oimè* and *ecco*) and to suggest the time by archaic grammar or idiom ('he hath other ware in which you deal'). But, when all is done, Nello speaks a language no one ever spoke and whose rhythms are not familiar to the author's ear as are the rhythms of English speech. We have only to compare a few sentences of an Englishman of similar social class, Mr Chubb, the innkeeper in *Felix Holt*, to recognize the devitalizing effect of Nello's language:

'Ah, sir', said Mr Chubb, with a certain bitterness in his smile, 'I've that sort of head that I've often wished I was stupider. I use things up, sir; I see into things a deal too quick. I eat my dinner, as you may say, at breakfast-time. That's why I hardly ever smoke a pipe. No sooner do I stick a pipe in my mouth than I puff and puff till it's gone before other folks are well lit; and then, where am I? I might as well have let it alone. In this world it's better not to be too quick. But you know what it is, sir.'[2]

Throughout *Romola* George Eliot is writing as though with her arm in a splint, the muscles which serve her best never have free play. The unsophisticated characters, Tessa and Monna Lisa for instance, suffer least, because, though she cannot give them the racy idiom of their English counterparts, the limited range of their minds prevents her from searching too strenuously for appropriate imagery. There is also more in common between the thought and therefore the language of simple people living three

---

[1] *Romola*, bk. I, ch. IV.   [2] *Felix Holt*, ch. XI.

centuries apart than between those whose minds are more fully furnished with the contemporary culture. But with no one in the book can she rely on the recollected sound of the spoken language. There is a similar impediment to her creation of the Florentine background. She has seen Florence in the nineteenth century, she has carefully studied the books and pictures that depict Florence in the fifteenth. But the visual impressions of fifteenth-century Florence are not embedded in her memory as are the visual impressions of English villages and country towns. Nor can she take anything for granted about her readers' familiarity with the scene of the book. Consequently, there is a continual effort when she describes, on the one hand to be accurate, and on the other to convey the scene she is reconstructing in considerable detail to her reader. There is a similar difference between *Romola* and the English books in the presentation of the ideas in the minds of her characters. She has researched into the history of thought in fifteenth-century Florence; she knows about the superstitions of the peasants, the beliefs and ascetic practices of the Dominican friars, the scepticism of the humanists, the political realism of Machiavelli and the cosmopolitan cynicism that could produce such a man as Tito Melema. She knows about all these, but she is intimate with none of them as she is with many varieties of thought and belief in nineteenth-century England, which she can recreate with an effortless spontaneity, because she has shared the feelings to which they give rise.

The centre as well as the circumference of the composition suffers from over-conscientiousness and the lack of a spontaneous creative impulse. The central theme is the study of the deterioration of Tito's character and the gradual unfolding and perfecting of Romola's. Since the book is called by her name it is likely that the author intended the interest to focus at least as much on her as on her husband. For most readers, however, Tito is both more convincing and more interesting, and this is surprising because Romola is essentially the same kind of woman as Maggie Tulliver or Dorothea Casaubon; that is to say she is the same kind of woman as George Eliot herself. Romola has, like her author, a keen receptive mind, a dependence on affection, and an impulse to hero-worship. She is the kind of woman George Eliot, for good reason, thoroughly understands. In *The Mill on the Floss* and in *Middlemarch* such characters are convincing as well as interesting. But in *Romola*, where the writer's conscious intelligence is continually on the alert to transpose her heroine into the world of fifteenth-century Florence, she does not persuade us to believe in her. The fact that Romola's mental development is the reverse of her own may have increased the necessity for continual conscious control. Romola is brought up in an atmosphere of strenuous, almost fanatical humanism and only comes into intimate contact with faith in the supernatural when her intelligence is mature. Moreover, the particular form that faith takes is not the one George Eliot had once herself accepted. The Roman Catholicism of Romola's brother and of Savonarola is a form of belief that George Eliot has had to study for the purposes of her book. The imaginative insight, springing from intimate sympathy, with which she communicates varieties of Protestant belief, ranging from the half-pagan superstitions of Dolly Winthrop to the bible-inspired devotion of Mr Tryan or of Mr Lyon, is replaced by an intelligent reconstruction of the comparable varieties of Catholic belief in fifteenth-century Florence. She succeeds better with the simple Christian-Paganism of Tessa (where the difference from a Protestant country-girl is hardly more than a difference in the symbols) than she does with Savonarola's belief and its impact on the mind of Romola. She can convey nothing, for instance, of the conflict in the mind of Savonarola when he finds himself in direct opposition to the Pope and excommunicated from the Church which is for him the embodiment of divine truth. (A similar failure of creative power occurs when she attempts to communicate the religious faith of Mordecai in *Daniel Deronda*.) The failure to breathe life into Romola is partly due to the author's inability to share the experiences that form her mind.

The presentation of Tito's character is more interesting, but here, too, something essential to success in creative writing is missed. The study of Tito is most painstaking and discerning—but it is an intellectual study. We are aware of a vigilant effort to be just to him and to inform us about those sides of his character which might win sympathy—but it is a sympathy we are never actually allowed to feel. Her frequent comments on Tito's motives are penetrating; the invention of his character is a vehicle through which she can express her own mature wisdom—but it is not the product of compassionate understanding. The three passages below illustrate the acuteness of her analysis of his character and the limitations of her method and of her attitude. The first occurs, after an elaborately analytical account of Tito's gradual self-persuasion, when he has finally decided to abandon the search for Baldassarre, his adoptive father who had rescued him when he was seven years old, and whom he now has money enough to ransom from slavery:

'Before I quit everything, and incur again all the risks of which I am even now weary, I must at least have a reasonable hope. Am I to spend my life in a wandering search? *I believe he is dead.* Cennini was right about my florins: I will place them in his hands to-morrow.'

When, the next morning, Tito put this determination into act he had chosen his colour in the game, and had given an inevitable bent to his wishes. He had made it impossible that he should not from henceforth desire it to be the truth that his father was dead; impossible that he should not be tempted to baseness rather than that the precise facts of his conduct should not remain forever concealed.

Under every guilty secret there is hidden a brood of guilty wishes, whose unwholesome infecting life is cherished by the darkness. The contaminating effect of deeds often lies less in the commission than in the consequent adjustment of our desires,—the enlistment of our self-interest on the side of falsity; as, on the other hand, the purifying influence of public confession springs from the fact that by it the hope in lies is forever swept away, and the soul recovers the noble attitude of simplicity.[1]

The commentary on the moral effects of Tito's crucial decision continues for another paragraph as long as the two quoted above,

[1] *Romola*, bk. I, ch. IX.

and the preponderance of discourse about the act over dramatic presentation of the act itself is typical of George Eliot's method with Tito throughout the novel.

The next extract indicates the nature of Tito's feelings about the little *contadina*, Tessa; it occurs when he is about to leave her after the mock marriage ceremony and it shows an aspect of Tito's character that might elicit sympathy:

'Perhaps I shall come again to you very soon, Tessa', he answered, rather dreamily, when they had moved away. He was thinking that when all the rest had turned their backs on him, it would be pleasant to have this little creature adoring him and nestling against him. The absence of presumptuous self-conceit in Tito made him feel all the more defenceless under prospective obloquy; he needed soft looks and caresses too much ever to be impudent.[1]

But this touch of nature in him leads on immediately to the crime of letting Tessa believe that she is really his wife. He had half intended to explain to her that the ceremony at the fair was a joke, but selfishness intervened. She says:

'I must go back once to the Madre, though, to tell her I brought the cocoons, and that I am married, and shall not go back again.'

Tito felt the necessity of speaking now; and in the rapid thought prompted by that necessity, he saw that by undeceiving Tessa he should be robbing himself of some at least of that pretty trustfulness which might by and by be his only haven from contempt. It would spoil Tessa to make her the least particle wiser or more suspicious.[1]

The third extract is taken from the opening of the dramatic scene that occurs when Tito finds that Baldassarre is in hiding in Tessa's cottage; he has the impulse to confess and be reconciled to his foster-father:

Tito longed to have his world once again completely cushioned with good-will, and longed for it the more eagerly because of what he had just suffered from the collision with Romola. It was not difficult to him to smile pleadingly on those whom he had injured, and offer to

[1] Ibid., bk. I, ch. XIV.

do them much kindness: and no quickness of intellect could tell him exactly the taste of that honey on the lips of the injured. The opportunity was there, and it raised an inclination which hemmed in the calculating activity of his thought.[1]

The presentation of Tito's character shows a subtle understanding of a type; when George Eliot exposes his motives the reader's mind consents; his shallow nature is everywhere consistently unfolded and, throughout the action, we watch corroding selfishness eating away potential good in him, but:

> Great literature...is the Forgiveness of Sin, and, when we find it becoming the Accusation of Sin, as in George Eliot, who plucks her Tito in pieces with as much assurance as if he had been clock-work, literature has begun to change into something else.[2]

This change only occurs in her novels when, for one reason or another, the creative impulse is overlaid by the intellectual. We are never allowed to discover Tito's nature by merely listening to him and observing what he does. At every turning-point in the story the flaw in his character is analysed and emphasized by the author. Consequently, as he becomes more and more entangled in his own deceits and forced to ever blacker acts of cowardice and cruelty, the reader has no sense of pitying discovery; compassion is swallowed up in the pride of sharing an intellectual triumph with the author as the sequence of events works out to its conclusion with mathematical inevitability.

When George Eliot chose the place and the time for the setting of her 'historical romance', she was doubtless attracted by the apparent similarities between the Florence of Savonarola and the England of Cardinal Newman. There was a similar cleavage of thought between the Renaissance humanists and the religious reformers as there was in the nineteenth century between the rationalists and the religious revivalists (whether High Anglican or Evangelical). In both periods there was strong hope and belief in the expansion of human knowledge and power;

---

[1] *Romola*, bk. II, ch. XXXIV.
[2] W. B. Yeats, *Ideas of Good and Evil*, 'At Stratford-on-Avon'.

there was also, among Christian believers in both periods, the recognition of a relaxation and even corruption in Church teaching and of a consequent deterioration in human conduct, resulting in a zealous desire to reform the Church. George Eliot's sceptical intelligence, combined with her compassionate understanding of religious experience, allowed her to sympathize both with Bardo's austere, fanatical rejection of the supernatural (comparable in its moral earnestness with that of such nineteenth-century agnostics as John Stuart Mill or Thomas Huxley) and with the religious zeal of Savonarola (comparable with that of Keble or Newman). She must have hoped to convey, in her novel, both the resemblance and the difference between the intellectual background of her own time and of fifteenth-century Florence. In fact she does not wholly succeed in doing either. She does not penetrate deeply enough into the minds of her principal characters to enable the reader to perceive both the recurrent motives of human thought and feeling and the specific pattern of thought and feeling that was shaped by all the historical circumstances. Her treatment of Savonarola suffers from her conscientious respect for history, as well as from her incomplete imaginative insight into his dilemma. She was too intellectually honest to invent him and too remote from him in experience to interpret convincingly the facts and documents by which she was circumscribed. At the two crises of his career which have their place in the novel, his shirking of the ordeal by fire and his solitary meditations after the torture, the reader is kept at a distance. We are given only what he is known to have said or written; we are not allowed to share his thinking or his feeling. This is inevitable; George Eliot would not feel free to go beyond her certain knowledge when she borrowed for fiction the name and story of a man who once lived and played his part in history. She had too much respect for human personality. Thus, once again, her creative impulse was paralysed, she was forced to rely on knowledge and thought. In her slight sketch of the young Machiavelli this is unimportant; the knowledge she has, and that she can assume her reader shares with her, warrants the general attitude to current political affairs that he is allowed to express. There is no attempt to create his personality. But Savonarola is a major figure in the composition, his personality affects both the background of her design, Florentine life and politics, and the foreground, the development of the characters and stories of Tito and Romola. It becomes essential that we should have a full imaginative understanding of the impact Savonarola makes and some understanding also of what it felt like to be Savonarola. But the historian's fidelity to the known fact and the novelist's fidelity to perceived truth come into conflict. He is neither intellectually understood and reconstructed as he might be by an historian who had no other end in view than to assemble, select from, and interpret the existing documents, nor is he invented with the confident insight into human character that George Eliot often had when she was not tied to fact and when she moved within a world she knew intimately and thoroughly understood.

It is probable that once she had chosen an historical subject from the remote past she was bound to fail. Her appeal is always to the serious reader, to the type of reader who would turn to memoirs, autobiographies and other contemporary records in search of historical truth. The imaginative artist must inevitably cast the shadow of his own *Zeitgeist* as well as of his own personality between the reader and the subject he paints. He cannot therefore supply the kind of historical knowledge which a reader would hope to arrive at through the records. Historical romance is another matter; its purpose is entertainment and the unfamiliar *décor* and manners of a remote period enhance the sense of escape and seem to justify events more vivid and characters more romantic than those of the present time. But, although George Eliot called her book an historical romance, she was not writing romance in this sense. Her purpose always, and her achievement when she succeeds, is the serious novel that enlarges the sympathies and exercises the ethical discriminations of the reader. Her success depends upon her creative impulse moving freely and confidently in the world of her own experience. Perhaps the great historical novels are all (like *War and Peace*) novels which do not reach further back than to the writer's own youth or to one generation earlier. The time immediately before the author's birth is the seed bed of his own experience; its social structure, its arts, manners and beliefs compose the environment in which the author's mind matures and from which his vision of life grows. The world of a writer's childhood is his home and the world of a remote past is a foreign country. The first is instinctively understood, the second is investigated with curiosity and discovered with surprise. If it is understood at all it is by an act of the intelligence, by knowledge gradually acquired and by a cautious use of analogies from his own times. Whether or no it be possible for a novelist to overcome these obstacles, George Eliot did not overcome them in *Romola*. There are memorable scenes in the book, there are some convincing characters, there is the merciless exposure of moral cowardice hardening into crime; but the novel is neither a successful reconstruction of fifteenth-century Florentine life nor a work of art capable of effecting what she herself thought necessary when she asserted that if art does not enlarge men's sympathies, it does nothing morally.[1]

[1] Cross, vol. II, p. 118. (Quoted from a letter to Charles Bray, 5 July 1859, with reference to her sympathy with 'that which is essentially human in all forms of belief'.)

CHAPTER IX

FELIX HOLT

AFTER the exhausting effort of writing *Romola* George Eliot did not begin another large-scale composition for two years. On 25 March 1865, she wrote in her journal:

I am in deep depression, feeling powerless. I have written nothing but beginnings since I finished a little article for the 'Pall Mall'....

But her creative life was only dormant and the depression was the prelude to activity; four days later the journal records, 'I have begun a novel'.[1] Fifteen months later *Felix Holt* was completed 'in a state of nervous excitement that had been making my head throb and my heart palpitate all the week before. As soon as I had finished it I felt well.'[2] In comparison with *Romola* this book was written with speed and ease and a sense of relative freedom and power communicates itself to the reader. It is good entertainment. In a sense it is, like *Romola*, an historical novel in that the subject involves a particular moment in the political history of England, thirty-five years before it was written. But it opens in 1830, the year in which the author was ten years old, and the scene is the English countryside of her childhood. The world in which the story moves is the world she knew so well, with its familiar class structure and the cleavage between the Church members and the Dissenters, which was as much social as doctrinal. It is a world she feels much less need to explain and describe than fifteenth-century Florence; instead she can allow her characters to reveal themselves in speech and action. She can communicate not only what they say, but the tone of their voice and the phrases and idioms that reflect their habit of mind. She can reproduce the pedantic, biblical phraseology of the dissenting minister, the standard English of the squirearchy, the communi-

[1] Cross, vol. II, p. 401.
[2] Ibid., p. 430. (In a letter to Mrs Congreve.)

cative irrelevances of the uneducated country woman or the 'refined accent and low quick monotonous tone' of the lady's maid. Pages of discourse, however wise and observant of abstract truths about human nature, cannot reveal personality as surely as does the dramatic method in convincing dialogue. A small-part character like Denner, the lady's maid, is more convincingly present in a single scene than Tito Melema in chapters of elaborate analysis. The reader co-operates in the discovery of her individuality. There is a scene early in the book, after the return of that son on whom all Mrs Transome's hopes were set, when Denner offers the shrewd, stoical wisdom she has garnered in her years of service to console her mistress. The reader discovers much about both women by being allowed to share this rare moment of expansiveness in their relationship. Denner is aware of all the disappointment Mrs Transome has felt in her first meeting with the son from whom she parted fifteen years before. To no one but Denner would Mrs Transome's pride allow her to reveal her own despairing fear of life:

... 'there's no pleasure for old women, unless they get it out of tormenting other people. What are your pleasures, Denner—besides being a slave to me?'

'Oh, there's pleasure in knowing one's not a fool, like half the people one sees about. And managing one's husband is some pleasure; and doing all one's business well. Why, if I've only got some orange flowers to candy, I shouldn't like to die till I see them all right. Then there's the sunshine now and then; I like that, as the cats do. I look upon it, life is like our game at whist, when Banks and his wife come to the still-room of an evening. I don't enjoy the game much, but I like to play my cards well, and see what will be the end of it; and I want to see you make the best of your hand, madam, for your luck has been mine these forty years now. But I must go and see how Kitty dishes up the dinner, unless you have any more commands.'

'No, Denner; I am going down immediately.'[1]

The all-important difference between *Felix Holt* and *Romola* is that the characters can define themselves in speech and act and

[1] *Felix Holt*, ch. 1.

that the reader is therefore not mainly dependent on the author to direct his opinion of them. Denner's forty years of loyal service becomes, in the light of such a glimpse of her character, a factor in the discovery of Mrs Transome. And the portrait of Mrs Transome is the most interesting achievement in the book.

The drama of her life was played out before the book began. She was unfaithful to her husband and had a son by the lawyer Jermyn, then a vigorous handsome youth and now coarsened by the years into *l'homme moyen sensuel*; he is a good husband and father, a successful business man, not more than averagely unscrupulous, but notably insensitive and impercipient. His energies are fully occupied with maintaining his professional position and the respect of his neighbours and his family. The reader first becomes aware of Mrs Transome as a woman who is cruel, bitter and proud. She has no pity for her senile husband, her love for Jermyn is dead and the whole force of her passionate nature is concentrated on her and Jermyn's son, known as Harold Transome. As the story of her past is gradually revealed and the reader discovers how her character has been formed and hardened, she elicits his compassion, not because the author pleads for it, but because the situation demands it.

In planning *Felix Holt* George Eliot seems to have had two themes in mind, the one political which would enable her to dramatize her own conclusions about the relation between constitutional reform and the life of the people, the other moral and similar in kind to the themes of all her novels, in that it concerns the way in which the development of character is determined by circumstance and by the choice made at some turning-point or crisis in an individual life. To combine these themes she chose the time of an election at Treby Magna, immediately preceding the first Reform Bill, and she associated all her main characters in some way with that election. At the centre of the political theme are the two contrasted Radicals, impelled by such different motives and opinions, Harold Transome and Felix Holt. Both play their part also in developing the moral theme. The private life of Felix is closely bound up with that of Esther and her foster-father, the little dissenting minister Mr Lyon. In order to establish a connection between the Transomes and Esther, George Eliot constructs an improbable and over-elaborate plot which involves one character who deliberately conceals his identity and two who are unaware who were their fathers. Ultimately, the mystery of Esther's paternity is unravelled and her claim to the Transome property established. This piece of detective fiction is not an end in itself, but the means of testing and developing Esther's character. It involves further demands on our credulity and it complicates the plot. It is necessary that Esther's mother should have settled in the same village as Christian who has concealed his own identity under that of Esther's dead father Bycliffe; further, Christian must conveniently lose his wallet containing papers which establish the truth about Bycliffe. Jermyn and Johnson each have their reasons for wanting to discover Bycliffe's heir, who has the legal right to the Transome estate. And, to complete this part of her story, George Eliot had to invent the tramp Tom Trounsem who, as Jermyn explains to Mrs Transome, is:

The last of the Thomas Transome line, by the purchase of whose interest your family got the title to the estate. Your title died with him. It was supposed that the line had become extinct before—and on that supposition the old Bycliffes founded their claim.

Tom Trounsem must be alive so that the Transomes may have won their claim against the Bycliffes before the book begins, and he has to die his timely and characteristic death (run over when drunk) so that Esther Bycliffe's claim may be found valid at the required moment. The plot necessitated the legal advice of Frederic Harrison; but, in spite of his co-operation, one contemporary critic doubted the validity of the legal situation described. In any case the plot is over-elaborate, bewilderingly complicated and disturbingly dependent on coincidence. The coincidences strain credulity and the complications distract the reader's attention from the problems in which the author is really interested. It is partly on account of this artificial plot that *Felix Holt* is not in the first rank of George Eliot's novels.

The political theme in *Felix Holt* is subordinate to the human theme. The book is not a political novel in the same sense as is, for instance, Disraeli's *Coningsby*; indeed the whole point of the political situation is that it illustrates George Eliot's belief that constitutional reform has only a very slight bearing on human happiness. In her third chapter she defines her own conception of the relation between social and political history and individual lives:

> These social changes in Treby parish are comparatively public matters, and this history is chiefly concerned with the private lot of a few men and women; but there is no private life which has not been determined by a wider public life, from the time when the primeval milkmaid had to wander with the wanderings of her clan, because the cow she milked was one of a herd which had made the pastures bare.

She was always keenly aware of the interconnection between the individual and society and it is illustrated in all her novels. The only peculiarity of *Felix Holt* in this respect is that she chooses a moment of history when the political life of England affected the normal life of the countryside in an unusually direct way. Her convincing picture of electioneering methods in 1830, and its effects on the simple population of an English country town enables her to illustrate the tenuous connection between an extended franchise and the democratic idea. Harold Transome chooses to stand as a Radical and to flout the family tradition, because the newer party appears to have a future before it and so to ensure him a career. His political agents, who have no political convictions, use any electioneering methods that fall within the law, including incitement to mob violence. Felix Holt, whose radicalism is of a wholly different character, sees that the root of the matter is not the extension of the franchise, and that genuinely representative government can only occur when the majority of men are sufficiently disinterested, well informed and clear-thinking to estimate the value of rival candidates or parties. Until such a time political power, whatever the constitution may be, will be liable to fall into the hands of such corrupt and self-seeking men as the agent, Johnson. Consequently Felix intends to remain a manual worker and to further his own political objective by educating the children of his fellow-workers. Felix is an idealized, romantic character because he has been invented to embody the author's ideas. In drawing him she was not contemplating and trying to discover a human being so much as inventing a mouthpiece for her own belief that the amelioration of man's lot will not follow directly upon improved political machinery.

For the moral theme of the book Mrs Transome and Esther Bycliffe are the principal characters. The first made a fatally self-indulgent choice many years before the opening of the story and throughout the book she reaps the bitter fruit of that choice by which her whole nature has been hardened; the second is offered in the course of the story a choice between, on the one hand, wealth, ease and the material refinements she keenly appreciates, all of which she can obtain by marrying her handsome, well-bred, but morally rather coarse suitor, Harold Transome (Jermyn's son), and, on the other, poverty and the simple life which will be hers if she accepts her other suitor, Felix Holt, whose moral refinement she recognizes beneath his uncouth manners. Mrs Transome has emerged from her wrong choice cold, embittered and unloved. Esther who is a charming and intelligent, but unconsciously selfish girl at the beginning of the book, develops selflessness and courage under the influence of the right choice, towards which she is gradually moving throughout the story. The juxtaposition and contrasting of these two women is an almost allegorical simplification of George Eliot's moral idea. The treatment is more subtle and serious than analysis suggests, because of the objective revelation of Mrs Transome. She is a more complex character than would suffice for the illustration of the theme. Nevertheless, the total composition is too schematic, too much the illustration of preconceived ideas for the novel to rank with George Eliot's highest achievements.

The surrounding characters who make up the social environment in which the story takes place are observed with the author's characteristic shrewdness and insight and with her habitual discernment of the varieties of moral scope. For instance, Felix's mother, Mrs Holt, is a thoroughly good woman within the narrow sphere of her endowment, but the goodness of her son has taken him beyond her range of vision; she can make no sense of his opposition to her making money out of the patent pills his father invented:

'...to say they're not good medicines, when they've been taken for fifty miles round by high and low, and rich and poor, and nobody speaking against 'em but Dr Lukin, it seems to me it's a flying in the face of Heaven; for if it was wrong to take the medicines, couldn't the blessed Lord have stopped it?'[1]

Or again, Mr Lingon, rector of Little Treby, is a good man, but Mr Lyon's wider conception of a minister's vocation is beyond his comprehension. Esther develops a personality whose moral range is much wider than Denner's, yet within her own compass, Denner is as good a woman:

A hard-headed godless little woman, but with a character to be reckoned on as you reckon on the qualities of iron.

The grades of badness are equally clearly discriminated. Jermyn is morally coarse and insensitive, yet his standards are higher than any Johnson can understand; Harold is corrupt by comparison with Felix Holt, but disinterested and virtuous by comparison with Jermyn. These distinctions emerge through speech and action without any need for the author to comment on them; the imaginative insight and sense of proportion from which they spring counterweighs the imperfections of the novel. The big scenes in the book, such as the mob riot in which Felix displays heroic rashness, the scene of the trial at which Esther declares her love for him and (the best written of them all) the scene in which Harold Transome is provoked to assault Jermyn

[1] *Felix Holt*, ch. IV.

with a riding whip and then discovers that he has struck his father, have a romantic quality on the verge of melodrama. They are excellent entertainment and they are essential to the composition: the principal performers in them act consistently with their characters, yet the dependence of the total effect on such scenes of dramatic tension, added to the improbabilities of the plot and the neatness of the central moral contrast, make the novel finally less convincing than George Eliot's major works. *Felix Holt* with its unmistakable hero and heroine and its near approach to a villain is the most romantic of George Eliot's books. If she was an old woman when she finished *Romola* she was rejuvenated when she wrote *Felix Holt*, for it has the same vitality as her early books with scenes of high comedy, such as Mrs Holt's visit to the Transomes, or the flight of the young curate from impending theological disputation with Mr Lyon, which bear comparison with some of the Poyser scenes in *Adam Bede* or the Pullet and Dodson scenes in *The Mill on the Floss*. She has also recovered and even increased her 'negative capability', she no longer dissects her evil-doers in ruthless sermons but allows Jermyn or Harold Transome to reveal their own limitations and elicit some compassion from the responsive reader. More important even than all this, the unfolding of Mrs Transome's character is subtle and convincing: she emerges into a clear light as the product of her own past as her story is gradually revealed and the reader discovers what lies behind her bitter pride. The merits of this novel are underrated when attention is too exclusively focussed on the intricate plot and the over-glamorous hero.

CHAPTER X

MIDDLEMARCH

THERE have been fluctuations in the critics' estimate of the value of *Middlemarch* in relation to George Eliot's other novels. It was a success on its first publication and George Eliot wrote in her journal, 1 January 1873:

> No former book of mine has been received with more enthusiasm—not even *Adam Bede*.[1]

During her lifetime it continued to be reckoned among the best of her novels. But when her total work was assessed immediately after her death it was the fashion to assert that she never recovered her creative vitality after *Romola* and that her best work is the work of her first period. In 1887, R. H. Hutton was exceptional in his opinion that:

> None of George Eliot's tales can compare with *Middlemarch* for delicacy of detail and completeness of finish—completeness as regards not only the individual figures but the whole picture of life delineated—and for the breadth of life brought within the field of the story.[2]

That opinion is shared by most modern critics, and to-day *Middlemarch* is commonly agreed to be the author's masterpiece.

Cross's *Life, Letters and Journals* supplies much information about the history of the composition and, in particular, the fact that the story of Lydgate and the story of Dorothea were conceived at different times and at first destined for separate works. *Middlemarch* was begun as a novel about Lydgate, a medical man of remarkable gifts whose potential services to mankind were impeded by circumstances. On 1 January 1869 George Eliot wrote in her journal: 'I have set myself many tasks for the year. I wonder how many will be accomplished?—a novel called

[1] Cross, vol. III, p. 191.
[2] *Modern Guides of English Thought.*

Middlemarch, a long poem on Timoleon, and several minor poems.'[1] On 19 July she wrote an introduction to the novel and on 23 July she records that she 'meditated characters for *Middlemarch*'.[2] On 5 August she finished a first chapter, but it was not the present first chapter; Dorothea had not yet become a part of her scheme. She was preoccupied with the medical theme in her book and was reading Rénouard's history of medicine. Various other entries in the journal tell of researches into medical matters and of meditating on the characters and environment of her story. On 2 August of the same year (1869) she wrote 'Began *Middlemarch* (the Vincy, Featherstone parts)'.[3] It is not until more than a year later (2 December 1870) that Dorothea is mentioned for the first time and then not in connection with the novel:

> I am experimenting in a story ('Miss Brooke') which I began without any very serious intention of carrying it out lengthily. It is a subject which has been recorded among my possible themes ever since I began to write fiction, but will probably take new shapes in the development. I am today at p. 44.[4]

By 31 December she records that she had written one hundred 'good printed pages' of this story.

It is at first surprising, in view of the impressive unity of the total effect of *Middlemarch* and the interdependence of the two main stories, to discover that they were not originally thought of as parts of one composition. It is much easier to imagine that the character of Adam Bede and the story of Hetty Sorrel were separate conceptions, or that the Stephen Guest episode in *The Mill on the Floss* developed after the novel about Maggie and her family was under way. And in *Daniel Deronda* the different treatment of the story of Gwendolen and the story of Daniel betrays the growth from separate roots. But the Lydgate and Dorothea themes in *Middlemarch* depend upon one another for their effect; the novel is a single organism and gives a remarkable impression of unity. The successful fusion is, however, not

---

[1] Cross, vol. III, p. 76. [2] Ibid., pp. 95–6
[3] Ibid., p. 97. [4] Ibid., p. 126.

so surprising when one remembers that the two stories and all
the surrounding circumstances and characters in *Middlemarch*
arise out of that vision of life to which George Eliot attained, in
its main features, before she began to write fiction; the vision
had matured with her experience and she had become increasingly
capable of expressing it in terms of creative fiction; both stories
embody aspects of that vision and, as in working on them she
perceived their implications more clearly, she recognized that they
were parts of a single pattern. In July 1871, by which time
Blackwood had received a considerable part of the manuscript,
she wrote to him:

I don't see how I can leave anything out, because I hope there is
nothing that will be seen to be irrelevant to my design, which is to
show the gradual action of ordinary causes rather than exceptional,
and to show this in some directions which have not been from time
immemorial the beaten path—the Cremorne walks and shows of fiction.
But the best intentions are good for nothing until execution has
justified them. And you know I am always compassed about with
fears. I am in danger in all my designs of parodying dear Goldsmith's
satire on Burke, and think of refining when novel reader's only think
of skipping.[1]

In the finished novel there is nothing 'irrelevant to the design':
although the book has the wealth of detail, the variety of characterization and the fertility of invention characteristic of the best
Victorian fiction, it has also the economy, proportion and unity
which has been the aim of serious novelists from the time of
Henry James. The unity is not merely an artificial contrivance, or
unity of plot, it arises out of singleness of vision and the many
characters and episodes in *Middlemarch* are interdependent aspects
of the central subject. The moral and intellectual qualities of each
character affect the reader's perception of the other characters
much as one object or one colour mass in a picture affects the
perception of every other.

The life of Middlemarch, the provincial town, is conveyed
with understanding and assurance comparable with the assured

confidence of Jane Austen in depicting the world she knew so well. The religious, social and economic history that lies behind and conditions that life is the same as that which conditioned George Eliot's own early development. The language in which the inhabitants of Middlemarch speak, with the idiom varying throughout the social scale, was familiar to her ear and she reproduced it with effortless mastery, and the pressure such an environment exercises on the individuals who compose it was a part of her own experience.

The original subject of the novel was the conditioning and limiting of the life of Lydgate by this environment. The novel was to have been the story of a young doctor with great gifts and a high ideal, frustrated by the circumstances in which he must work and by the human mixture of faults and virtues in his own nature. Apparently George Eliot had planned the treatment of this subject in considerable detail before she saw the Miss Brooke story as related to it. Lydgate's promise, the promise of a man of exceptional moral and intellectual gifts, was unfulfilled partly because of the obstructive stupidity of the people among whom he worked and the various cross-currents of religious and political prejudice, professional jealousy and economic difficulty which can impede the progress of medical science. But unfulfilment was to be partly also the result both of positive and negative qualities in his own character. In the finished novel the reader is allowed to suppose that he might have surmounted all the obstacles if he had not married Rosamond Vincy. His marriage is a consequence of arrogance and of what George Eliot calls 'spots of commonness' in him:

Lydgate's conceit was of the arrogant sort, never simpering, never impertinent, but massive in its claims and benevolently contemptuous. He would do a great deal for noodles, being sorry for them, and feeling quite sure that they could have no power over him: he had thought of joining the Saint Simonians when he was in Paris, in order to turn them against some of their own doctrines. All his faults were marked by kindred traits, and were those of a man who had a fine baritone, whose clothes hung well upon him, and who even in his ordinary gestures had an air of inbred distinction. Where then lay the spots of commonness?...How could there be any commonness in a man so well-bred, so ambitious of social distinction, so generous and unusual in his views of social duty?...Lydgate's spots of commonness lay in the complexion of his prejudices which, in spite of noble intention and sympathy, were half of them such as are found in ordinary men of the world: that distinction of mind which belonged to his intellectual ardour, did not penetrate his feeling and judgment about furniture, or women, or the desirability of its being known (without his telling) that he was better born than other country surgeons.[1]

The streak of arrogance and of snobbishness, venial faults such as mar the best of men and women, are a part of the reason why he chooses the pretty, refined product of Miss Lemon's finishing school, Rosamond Vincy, without either expecting or wishing to find in her an intellect or aspirations to match his own. But good qualities in his nature are also part of the reason; particularly his compassionate heart; it is the sight of Rosamond's distress and genuine tears when she thinks she has failed to capture him that bring about the declaration:

That moment of naturalness was the crystallising feather-touch: it shook flirtation into love.[2]

And Lydgate's final capitulation to circumstances, after the exposure of Bulstrode and all that it involves, is the result of his loyalty and tenderness for the wife he no longer loves, much more than of defects in his nature. But though all this may have been clearly foreseen by George Eliot in the first year of her work on the novel, before the Miss Brooke story became amalgamated with it, the light in which the reader now sees this part of the subject emanates in a high degree from the other story.

The story that had been 'recorded among possible themes' since she began to write fiction is that of a woman endowed with qualities of mind and heart and a passionate desire to serve her

---

[1] *Middlemarch*, bk. ii, ch. xv.
[2] Ibid., bk. iii, ch. xxxi.

kind, which make her comparable with St Theresa, but whose opportunities are confined by the conditions of a well-to-do provincial English girl in the nineteenth century. Clearly the subject, like the Lydgate subject, arises out of George Eliot's perception that historical circumstances, particularly in her own century, often result in a small proportion of achievement in comparison with endowment. It is not surprising that she discovered Middlemarch to be the right setting for Miss Brooke as well as for Lydgate. Both characters have to adapt themselves to the demands and conventions of provincial society of the period. For the man a career is open which promises the fulfilment of his ideal, though he is hedged about by the time and place in which he enters on that career. Marriage is irrelevant to it, except in so far as it will limit his economic freedom and, on this account, he intends to avoid or at least postpone it. For the woman, on the contrary, marriage is the only conceivable career. Consequently, she chooses a mate in the hope of finding, through him, her opportunity to serve humanity. She hopes to find a husband with gifts of character and intelligence superior to her own. And so, when Dorothea Brooke receives Casaubon's stilted letter of proposal:

How could it occur to her to examine the letter, to look at it critically as a profession of love? Her whole soul was possessed by the fact that a fuller life was opening before her: she was a neophyte about to enter on a higher grade of initiation. She was going to have room for the energies which stirred uneasily under the dimness and pressure of her own ignorance and the petty peremptoriness of the world's habits.

Now she would be able to devote herself to large yet definite duties; now she would be allowed to live continually in the light of a mind that she could reverence. This hope was not unmixed with the glow of proud delight—the joyous maiden surprise that she was chosen by the man whom her admiration had chosen. All Dorothea's passion was transfused through a mind struggling towards an ideal life; the radiance of her transfigured girlhood fell on the first object that came within its level.[1]

[1] Ibid., bk. I, ch. v.

That object happened to be Edward Casaubon, just as Rosamond Vincy happened to be the object that answered Lydgate's preconception of a restful, ornamental creature, whose unexacting companionship he could enjoy in his hours of leisure. The tragic outcome of the one marriage is the counterpart of the tragic outcome of the other. It seems not only fitting but necessary to the full understanding of their predicament that Dorothea and Lydgate should form part of a single pattern. But, in her treatment of the two stories, when she had joined them, George Eliot did not stop short at juxtaposition and contrast. The relation between Lydgate and Dorothea is a principal factor in the development of Lydgate's character; the ennobling of Lydgate and purgation of his 'spots of commonness', which partly compensates for the tragic waste, is affected by his contact with Dorothea. After his first meeting with her Lydgate reflects:

She is a good creature—that fine girl—but a little too earnest. . . . It is troublesome to talk to such women. They are always wanting reasons, yet they are too ignorant to understand the merits of any question, and usually fall back on their moral sense to settle things after their own taste.[1]

A little later he considers her in comparison with Rosamond Vincy and decides that:

She did not look at things from the proper feminine angle. The society of such women was about as relaxing as going from your work to teach the second form, instead of reclining in a paradise with sweet laughs for bird-notes and blue eyes for a heaven.[2]

Lydgate has a long and hard road to travel before he appreciates the value of such a woman as Dorothea and the various places in the story at which their paths intersect are essential to the unfolding and presentation of his character. Furthermore, he is as essential a part of her story as she is of his. He is often an agent in those parts of the action of the novel that concern her, either because of his medical relations with Casaubon, or his financial relations with Bulstrode, or his social relations with Ladislaw.

[1] *Middlemarch*, bk. I, ch. X.   [2] Ibid., bk. I, ch. XI.

All this belongs to the machinery of construction and any novelist competent to construct a fairly elaborate plot would know how to interconnect the main characters with similar economy. The relationship between the two operates also at a deeper level. Lydgate is an essential factor in the development of Dorothea's character, events connected with him help to mature her nature and to communicate the whole of it to the reader. The portrait of Dorothea is not complete until we have witnessed her courageous faith in him when the rest of her world suspect him of accepting a bribe to shelter a murderer, and her mission of mercy to his wife when she returns to Rosamond in the full belief that Ladislaw is her lover and that Rosamond has therefore destroyed her own last hope of personal happiness. Thus the two themes which George Eliot at first thought of as the material for two separate stories become parts of a single whole and together create the central life of the book as we know it.

Lydgate and Dorothea together are the vehicle for the main theme in *Middlemarch*. The compromise each ultimately makes between the life to which they aspired and the life the conditions permit symbolizes the conception at the heart of the book.

But George Eliot was not confined by her central theme; her creative imagination operated freely in this novel, disciplined but not inhibited by the requirements of artistic economy and proportion. Everything in the book is relevant to the design, but nothing is merely relevant. For instance, for the presentation of the theme it suffices that the marriage partners of Lydgate and Dorothea should be a worldly, unintelligent coquette and an egotist whose pretensions to genius are false. But both characters are in fact complex and intrinsically interesting far in excess of this requirement. Rosamond's moral stupidity, her incapacity to see beyond her own pitifully inadequate standards, is painted with penetrating insight and is frighteningly true to life. Few scenes in fiction are more convincing, or more effectively enraging, than that between Rosamond and her husband when she reveals how she has frustrated his plan to free them from debt.[1] Her unshake-

[1] Ibid., bk. VII, ch. LXV.

able assurance that she alone is the aggrieved party—and it is her characteristic attitude of mind—elicits a horrified compassion not only for her husband, but for her own narrowness of vision. The last words about her in the book sum up a conception of her character that has been formed in the reader's mind by degrees with little need for the author's directing commentary. George Eliot seems to know intuitively what Rosamond will say and do on every occasion and, though we are constantly surprised at the degree of her impercipience and the particular twist it takes, we are never in doubt of the consistency of the portrait. By the end we scarcely need to be told that:

Rosamond never committed a second compromising indiscretion. She simply continued to be mild in her temper, inflexible in her judgment, disposed to admonish her husband, and able to frustrate him by stratagem.

The impotent rage she arouses in her husband is shared by the reader, but while Lydgate's pity and tenderness towards her are the aftermath of love and the outcome of his own sense of responsibility, the reader is only compassionate in so far as he recognizes her limitations. Rosamond is never depicted as deliberately wicked, she is merely incapable of understanding any values more altruistic than her own. The most brilliant stroke of creative genius in her portrait occurs in the scene between her and Dorothea.[1] Cross informs us how little, according to his wife's own account, that scene was consciously contrived:

She told me that, in all that she considered her best writing, there was a 'not herself' which took possession of her, and that she felt her own personality to be merely the instrument through which this spirit, as it were, was acting. Particularly she dwelt on this with regard to the scene in *Middlemarch* between Dorothea and Rosamond, saying that, although she always knew they had, sooner or later, to come together, she kept the idea resolutely out of her mind until Dorothea was in Rosamond's drawing-room. Then, abandoning herself to the inspiration of the moment, she wrote the whole scene exactly as it

[1] *Middlemarch*, bk. VIII, ch. LXXXI.

stands, without alteration or erasure, in an intense state of excitement and agitation, feeling herself entirely possessed by the feelings of the two women. Of all the characters she had attempted, she found Rosamond, the most difficult to sustain.[1]

In that scene, at a moment when George Eliot had abandoned conscious intellectual control and given free rein to her imagination, Rosamond behaves against the current of her nature: she is momentarily actuated, at any rate in part, by a generous impulse. This abnormality is prepared for by, and is the convincing consequence of, the preceding scene with Ladislaw. Dorothea has found them together and has left the house under the impression, almost inevitable in the circumstances, that Ladislaw is Rosamond's lover. Ladislaw, realizing fully the misapprehension under which Dorothea has gone away and hopeless of any possibility of dispelling it, turns on Rosamond and forces her to see, as she has never done before, herself mirrored in the consciousness of another:

Rosamond, while these poisoned weapons were being hurled at her, was almost losing the sense of her identity, and seemed to be waking into some new terrible existence. She had no sense of chill resolute repulsion, of reticent self-justification such as she had known under Lydgate's most stormy displeasure: all her sensibility was turned into a bewildering novelty of pain—she felt a new terrified recoil under a lash never experienced before. What another nature felt in opposition to her own was being burnt and bitten into her consciousness. When Will had ceased to speak she had become an image of sickened misery: her lips were pale, and her eyes had a tearless dismay in them.[2]

When Dorothea comes to her the second time, Rosamond is still under the influence of this experience: Ladislaw has broken through the almost impregnable defence of her self-complacency:

...she was under the first great shock that had shattered her dream-world in which she had been easily confident of herself and critical of others;...[3]

[1] Cross, vol. III, p. 424.
[2] *Middlemarch*, bk. VIII, ch. LXXVIII.
[3] Ibid., ch. LXXXI.

It will not be long before the dream-world walls her in again; but at the moment when Dorothea—unmindful of her own impaired dream—comes back to fulfil her intention of restoring Rosamond's confidence in her husband, she finds her without her usual defences. She tells Dorothea the truth about her own one-sided flirtation with Ladislaw, and that when Dorothea found them together: 'He was telling me how he loved another woman, that I might know he could never love me....' Rosamond has her one generous gesture and, even before it is completed, we see her begin to re-establish her self-confidence.

The portrait of Casaubon is no less complete than that of Rosamond. He is far from being merely a necessary factor in the unfolding of Dorothea's personality and story. His character is intrinsically interesting and convincing; ultimately he wins the compassion of the reader as well as of his wife. At first, while she thirstily follows the mirage of an intellectual hero, the reader sees only a formal, egotistical pedant. Gradually, Casaubon's inner consciousness is revealed, his corroding envy, his unsuccessful fight against recognizing the vanity of the researches on which he has spent his life, his hopeless sickness of body and mind. Casaubon causes almost as much misery as Rosamond, and with more evil intention. But his portrait, unlike hers, evokes the sense of tragic waste. He has a better endowment than she has and is unlike her in his capacity for prolonged suffering. The wall he erects between himself and others is a deliberate repudiation of pity; within it he is not successfully self-deceived as she is.

Although in this novel George Eliot's treatment of human personality and her care for the unity of her design are those of a modern novelist, the construction of *Middlemarch* is in the nineteenth-century tradition. An elaborate plot interlocks the various groups of characters and is carefully devised for that purpose. Three figures, the miser Featherstone, his frog-faced natural son Rigg, and Rigg's step-father, the drunken scoundrel Raffles, exist for the plot only and are of no intrinsic interest. They are vivid, semi-grotesque creatures who would not be out of place in the world Dickens creates. George Eliot gives each of them just enough reality to compel belief for the moment and has no further interest in them. They are creatures of farce or melo-drama; but they are indispensable to the full story of the fore-ground characters in the novel. Featherstone (out of mere malice and the joy of disappointing all his expectant relatives) leaves his property to Rigg. Rigg's stepfather, Raffles, is attracted to Middlemarch in consequence. Thereby he becomes the means of exposing the past life of Bulstrode and its connection with Ladislaw's parents. It is the blackmailing drunkard, Raffles, who occasions not only the full display of Bulstrode's character, but the whole episode of Lydgate's disgrace. These three grotesques are mere puppets; they are tools which the author uses with skill and discards when they have fulfilled their purpose.

This aspect of the novel is a consciously contrived unifying agent, but *Middlemarch* has another kind of unity which is not contrived but grows out of the author's singleness of vision. Bulstrode, who plays his essential part in the contrivance, is a fully realized character whose existence in the Middlemarch world has an effect on the reader's total impression over and above his function in the plot. His portrait is a serious study of hypocrisy (different in kind from, for instance, Dickens's epitomizing of that quality in Pecksniff). Like the other major characters in this novel he is not explained by the author, but gradually discovered as the history advances, and only seen in a full light when his past is revealed in the course of the action. When he first enters the story he has for years successfully imposed himself on the inhabitants of Middlemarch as an exceptionally pious and philanthropic citizen. But he has never wholly succeeded in deceiving himself. His conscience is still painfully active, though it has been warped by his prolonged effort to compromise between worldly ambition and genuine religious zeal. The root of his hypocrisy is his continual striving for self-deception. In the inner pattern of the novel the relation between this man and his wife is as important as are his relations with Lydgate. Mrs Bulstrode, a worthy, common place woman, as limited in her mental equipment as is her agreeable sister Mrs

Vincy (Rosamond's mother), has her moment of tragic grandeur in which she rises to the moral plane on which Dorothea habitually moves. This occurs when her brother-in-law Vincy tells her of her husband's public disgrace and of the extent, known and suspected, of his offence:

She locked herself in her room. She needed time to get used to her maimed consciousness, her poor lopped life, before she could walk steadily to the place allotted her. A new searching light had fallen on her husband's character, and she could not judge him leniently: the twenty years in which she had believed in him and venerated him by virtue of his concealments came back with particulars that made them seem an odious deceit. He had married her with that bad past life hidden behind him and she had no faith left to protest his innocence of the worst that was imputed to him. Her honest ostentatious nature made the sharing of a merited dishonour as bitter as it could be to any mortal.

But this imperfectly-taught woman, whose phrases and habits were an odd patchwork, had a loyal spirit within her. The man whose prosperity she had shared through nearly half a life, and who had unvaryingly cherished her—now that punishment had befallen him it was not possible to her in any sense to forsake him. There is a forsaking which still sits at the same board and lies on the same couch with the forsaken soul, withering it the more by unloving proximity. She knew, when she locked her door, that she should unlock it ready to go down to her unhappy husband and espouse his sorrow, and say of his guilt, I will mourn and not reproach. But she needed time to gather up her strength; she needed to sob out her farewell to all the gladness and pride of her life. When she had resolved to go down, she prepared herself by some little acts which might seem mere folly to a hard onlooker; they were her way of expressing to all spectators visible or invisible that she had begun a new life in which she embraced humiliation. She took off all her ornaments and put on a plain black gown, and instead of wearing her much-adorned cap and large bows of hair, she brushed her hair down and put on a plain bonnet-cap, which made her look suddenly like an early Methodist.

Bulstrode, who knew that his wife had been out and had come in saying that she was not well, had spent the time in an agitation equal to hers. He had looked forward to her learning the truth from others, and had acquiesced in that probability, as something easier to him than any confession. But now that he imagined the moment of her knowledge come, he awaited the result in anguish. His daughters had been obliged to consent to leave him, and though he had allowed some food to be brought to him, he had not touched it. He felt himself perishing slowly in unpitied misery. Perhaps he should never see his wife's face with affection in it again. And if he turned to God there seemed to be no answer but the pressure of retribution.

It was eight o'clock in the evening before the door opened and his wife entered. He dared not look up at her. He sat with his eyes bent down, and as she went towards him she thought he looked smaller—he seemed so withered and shrunken. A movement of new compassion and old tenderness went through her like a great wave, and putting one hand on his which rested on the arm of the chair, and the other on his shoulder, she said, solemnly but kindly—

'Look up, Nicholas.'[1]

The Bulstrodes are intrinsically interesting and important characters in the novel, and the reader's attitude towards them has that quality of compassion which George Eliot elicits for most of the main characters in *Middlemarch*. But, in addition to this, the episode of Bulstrode's exposure acts as a touchstone testing the value of all those who come into contact with it. It reveals the alloy in Lydgate's nature and the pure metal of Caleb Garth who, with characteristic simplicity, humility and inflexible integrity resigns the appointment as managing agent of Stone Court, which he had recently accepted with so much happiness because it offered precisely the work he enjoyed and at which he excelled, as well as removing all his financial worries. As soon as he feels bound to suspect the source of Bulstrode's wealth he knows what he must do:

'You have been led to this, I apprehend, by some slanders concerning me uttered by that unhappy creature',[2] said Bulstrode, anxious now to know the utmost.

'That is true. I can't deny that I act upon what I heard from him.'

'You are a conscientious man, Mr Garth—a man, I trust, who feels himself accountable to God. You would not wish to injure me by being too ready to believe a slander', said Bulstrode, casting about for

---

[1] *Middlemarch*, bk. VIII, ch. LXXIV.   [2] Raffles.

pleas that might be adapted to his hearer's mind. 'That is a poor reason for giving up a connection which I think I may say will be mutually beneficial.'

'I would injure no man if I could help it', said Caleb; 'even if I thought God winked at it. I hope I should have a feeling for my fellow-creature. But, sir—I am obliged to believe that this Raffles has told me the truth. And I can't be happy in working with you, or pro-fiting by you. It hurts my mind. I must beg you to seek another agent.'[1]

Middlemarch is George Eliot's supreme achievement: while its characters are at least as various and as deeply studied as any she has created, they are more perfectly combined into a single whole than those in any other of her novels. Nothing here is irrelevant or over-elaborated. Each character reveals itself in the sequence of events with such consistency with its own nature as wins the reader's complete assent. The imagination of the author seems to be wholly engaged in discovering what each one would be doing or saying in the special circumstances of each scene or episode. And yet every one of them has a function in the whole design. Our final apprehension of the moral quality of Lydgate and Dorothea depends upon our seeing them in relation to all the others. The flawless integrity and unworldliness of the Garth family offsets the streak of snobbishness and materialism in Lydgate. The unostentatious kindliness of Mr Farebrother offsets Lydgate's more arrogant virtue; little Miss Noble's small charities done by stealth are a comical counterpart of Dorothea's unsatisfied thirst to do good. It is not likely that these particular juxtapositions were consciously intended by the author, but they, and others of the same kind, occur because all the characters who make up the world in which Lydgate and Dorothea live are the product of the same vision of life. We are compelled throughout the book to see as George Eliot saw. The weaving of the plot and the part each character plays in it is the result of her conscious purpose and planning. But the part each character plays in producing the total impression evoked by the novel is the result

[1] *Middlemarch*, bk. VII, ch. LXIX.

of her creative power. She could divest herself of her own individual characteristics and preoccupations and identify herself with all these human beings, limiting herself to their knowledge, their temperament and their circumstances. There is less direct intercourse between author and reader than in most of her novels because there is less need for it. She has only to compel our attention to the world she has created; its inner coherence is the result of her own coherent vision.

Some critics, both in George Eliot's day and in our own, have found fault with her conception of Ladislaw and of his relation to Dorothea. In September 1873, George Eliot wrote to John Blackwood:

> When I was at Oxford, in May, two ladies came up to me after dinner: one said, 'How could you let Dorothea marry *that* Casaubon?' The other, 'Oh, I understand her doing that, but why did you let her marry the other fellow, whom I cannot bear?' Thus two 'ardent admirers' wished that the book had been quite different from what it is.[1]

Whatever else may be thought of either Casaubon or Ladislaw, Dorothea's feelings about them are an inseparable part of the author's idea of her personality. Furthermore, it is at least probable that the impression made by the presentation of a character is intended by the author from whom it derives. For instance, George Eliot wrote about *The Mill on the Floss*:

> Letters drop in from time to time giving me words of strong encouragement—especially about *The Mill*; so that I have reason to be cheerful, and to believe that where one has a large public, one's words must hit their mark. If it were not for that, special cases of misinterpretation might paralyse me. For example one critic attributes to me a disdain of Tom; as if it were not *my* respect for Tom which infused itself into my reader,—as if he could have respected Tom if I had not painted him with respect; the exhibition of the right on both sides being the very soul of my intention in the story....[2]

In so far as the responsive reader feels that Ladislaw is not quite good enough for Dorothea it is probable that George Eliot's feeling has 'infused itself' into him. Her theme is the adjustment

[1] Cross, vol. III, p. 213.   [2] Cross, vol. II, p. 296.

of the aspiring individual to the inhibiting conditions of an actual social world. Marriage with Ladislaw is not meant to be the fulfilment of Dorothea's youthful dreams. Her first marriage was a tragic mistake—her imaginary portrait of Casaubon as a modern Milton was an illusion. Subsequently compassion for him took the place of hero-worship and formed a sufficient bond to ensure her loyalty. Her second marriage is an improvement on the first, because its basis is an appreciation of the man as he is; their love for each other comprises mutual sympathy, understanding and respect. Casaubon chose Dorothea, as she chose him, because each thought the other corresponded to a pre-existing idea in their own mind. But Dorothea invents no fiction about Ladislaw nor he about her; they respect one another for what they discern in one another. There are two relevant questions for the reader: first, whether the author conveys a sufficiently rounded impression of Ladislaw to compel belief in his existence, and secondly, whether she makes it credible that Dorothea would love him. If a negative answer is given it is usually to the second question. The reader discerns faults, weaknesses or irritating tricks in Ladislaw which, he supposes, would alienate her. Ladislaw is dilettante, that is to say that (in his early twenties) he cannot choose a career and settle down to it. In the grip of his passion for Dorothea he vacillates about leaving Middlemarch and continually finds an excuse to return. He offends and perplexes Middlemarch society in general by his easy, unconventional manners; to them he seems like a foreigner; they are not surprised to learn that his father was a Jewish pawnbroker. Perhaps George Eliot has succeeded so well in making her readers inhabit Middlemarch that they too readily adopt the Middlemarch point of view. But she has provided a counterbalancing impression. The discerning characters, those less bounded by the conventional standards of the provincial town, such as Lydgate or Mr Farebrother, are not offended by Ladislaw's manners. Mr Farebrother's sister, the admirable little old lady, Miss Noble, almost worships him because of his kindness to ragged children and his courtesy to herself. He has certain qualities which were particularly likely to attract Dorothea after her experience with Casaubon. He is spontaneous and unselfconscious; he responds to beauty in art or nature and to nobility in human character with romantic ardour. His intelligence is quick and gay—a happy contrast to Casaubon's ponderous learning. His nature is in many ways complementary to her own. Certainly George Eliot did not intend us to share Sir James Chettam's view that their marriage was a disaster.

The reader's feeling about this marriage has a bearing on another common criticism of *Middlemarch*, that it is, in R. H. Hutton's words:

Profoundly melancholy both in aim and in execution.

In a sense this is obviously true, but it is not the whole truth about the book. An important part of George Eliot's intention in *Middlemarch*, as elsewhere, was to arouse compassion for the human predicament.

If art does not enlarge men's sympathies it does nothing morally,[1]

she wrote in 1859, and, from the beginning of her career she hoped to enlarge them and particularly to elicit sympathy for the unspectacular sorrows of ordinary men and women. In *Middlemarch* itself, commenting on Dorothea's unhappiness in Rome, on her honeymoon with Casaubon, she wrote:

Some discouragement, some faintness of heart at the new real future which replaces the imaginary, is not unusual, and we do not expect people to be deeply moved by what is not unusual. That element of tragedy which lies in the very fact of frequency, has not yet wrought itself into the coarse emotion of mankind; and perhaps our frames could hardly bear much of it. If we had a keen vision and feeling of all ordinary human life, it would be like hearing the grass grow and the squirrel's heart beat, and we should die of that roar which lies on the other side of silence. As it is, the quickest of us walk about well wadded with stupidity.[2]

[1] Cross, vol. II, p. 118.
[2] *Middlemarch*, bk. II, ch. XX.

In so far as *Middlemarch* removes some of that wadding and opens our ears to normal human sorrow, it is a melancholy book. The tragic waste of Lydgate, the incomplete fulfilment of Dorothea's promise, the moral degradation of Bulstrode, the disappointment of Farebrother when Mary Garth gives herself to Fred Vincy, who needs her more than he does, but deserves her less—all these are melancholy as certainly as they are lifelike. But it is doubtful whether the sorrow in the book outweighs the happiness. Against these woes must be set the various happy or contented lives; the pleasant ménage of Mr Farebrother with his mother and sisters; the satisfactory marriage of Celia and Sir James Chettam; the suitable and comfortable relationship of Mr and Mrs Vincy, which creates a tolerable happiness in spite of their worries over their children; Fred Vincy's improvement under the Garth influence and his happiness with Mary; the relation between Mr and Mrs Garth, in which a flawless union has compensated for many material anxieties, the satisfactory marriage of that odd pair, the Cadwalladers. All these counterbalancing pictures of normal human content, including (a subject rarely treated in fiction) happiness in the day's work (particularly emphasized in the portrait of Caleb Garth) together prevent the total effect of the book from being gloomy. Moreover, the reader is constantly delighted and enlivened by the author's gift for comedy which is only a little less evident here than in *Adam Bede* or *The Mill on the Floss*. It just avoids caricature in the portrait of Mr Brooke or of Mrs Cadwallader, and it establishes the character of old Mrs Farebrother in a single scene. The occasion is the introduction of Lydgate to the family circle and it is the first appearance of Mrs Farebrother in the novel:

Mrs Farebrother welcomed the guest with a lively formality and precision. She presently informed him that they were not often in want of medical aid in that house. She had brought up her children to wear flannel and not to over-eat themselves, which last habit she considered the chief reason why people needed doctors. Lydgate pleaded for those whose fathers and mothers had over-eaten themselves, but Mrs Farebrother held that view of things dangerous: Nature was more just than that; it would be easy for any felon to say that his ancestors ought to have been hanged instead of him. If those who had bad fathers and mothers were bad themselves, they were hanged for that. There was no need to go back on what you couldn't see.

'My mother is like old George the Third,' said the Vicar, 'she objects to metaphysics.'

'I object to what is wrong, Camden. I say, keep hold of a few plain truths, and make everything square with them. When I was young, Mr Lydgate, there never was any question about right and wrong. We knew our catechism, and that was enough; we learned our creed and our duty. Every respectable Church person had the same opinions. But now, if you speak out of the Prayer-book itself, you are liable to be contradicted.'

'That makes rather a pleasant time of it for those who like to maintain their own point', said Lydgate.

'But my mother always gives way', said the Vicar, slyly.

'No, no, Camden, you must not lead Mr Lydgate into a mistake about *me*. I shall never show that disrespect to my parents, to give up what they taught me. Any one may see what comes of turning. If you change once, why not twenty times?'

'A man might see good arguments for changing once, and not see them for changing again', said Lydgate, amused with the decisive old lady.

'Excuse me there. If you go upon arguments, they are never wanting, when a man has no constancy of mind. My father never changed, and he preached plain moral sermons without arguments, and was a good man—few better. When you get me a good man made out of arguments, I will get you a good dinner with reading the cookery-book. That's my opinion, and I think anybody's stomach will bear me out.'[1]

The scene is not only amusing, it has depth of understanding, shrewdness of observation and the sure ear for dialogue which went to the making of Mrs Poyser or of Maggie's aunts, and whose inevitable maiming in *Romola* detracts so much from that book. Presently Mrs Farebrother praises her son at the expense of the

---

[1] *Middlemarch*, bk. II, ch. XVII.

other candidate for the hospital chaplaincy, Bulstrode's protégé, Mr Tyke; Camden interposes:

'A mother is never partial.... What do you think Tyke's mother says about him?'

'Ah, poor creature! what indeed?' said Mrs Farebrother, her sharpness blunted for the moment by her confidence in maternal judgments. 'She says the truth to herself, depend upon it.'[1]

In *Middlemarch* George Eliot presents a world too various and too absorbingly interesting and amusing for the total effect of the book to be melancholy—the selection of experience in it represents the typical sorrows of ordinary human beings, but it represents no less vividly the common human joys. And, as with all successful works of art, there is an overbalance of delight which comes from the contemplation of work well done.

[1] *Middlemarch*, bk. ii, ch. xvii.

CHAPTER XI

DANIEL DERONDA

THE first mention of *Daniel Deronda* in Cross's *Life* is in George Eliot's journal for 1875. But the originating impulse from which one part of her last novel developed was an experience that occurred three years before. A month after the completion of *Middlemarch*, October 1872, she wrote to Mrs Cross (mother of her future husband) from Homburg:

The air, the waters, the plantations here, are all perfect—'only man is vile'. I am not fond of denouncing my fellow-sinners, but gambling being a vice I have no mind to, it stirs my disgust even more than my pity. The sight of the dull faces bending round the gaming tables, the raking up of money, and the flinging of the coins towards the winners by the hard-faced croupiers, the hateful, hideous women staring at the board like stupid monomaniacs—all this seems to me the most abject presentation of mortals grasping after something called good, that can be seen on the face of this little earth. Burglary is heroic compared with it;[1]

and on 4 October to John Blackwood:

The Kursaal is to me a hell, not only for the gambling but for the light and heat of the gas, and we have seen enough of its monstrous hideousness. There is very little dramatic *Stoff* to be picked up by watching or listening. The saddest thing to be witnessed is the play of a young lady, who is only twenty-six years old, and is completely in the grasp of this mean, money-making demon. It made me cry to see her young fresh face among the hags and brutally stupid men around her.[2]

Sterile disgust which saw in the gamblers nothing but a symbol of human greed was fertilized by the strong impulse of pity for an individual gambler. The total experience bore fruit in one of

[1] Cross, vol. III, pp. 169–70.   [2] Ibid., p. 171.

the most interesting of her studies of human character, Gwendolen Harleth. The novel opens with Daniel Deronda watching
a young girl gambling in a 'scene of dull, gas-poisoned ab-
sorption'...

suddenly he felt the moment become dramatic. His attention was
arrested by a young lady who, standing at an angle not far from him,
was the last to whom his eyes travelled. She was bending and speaking
English to a middle-aged lady seated at play beside her; but the next
instant she returned to her play, and showed the full height of a
graceful figure, with a face which might possibly be looked at without
admiration, but could hardly be passed with indifference.[1]

It was three years after she herself had witnessed such a scene
that George Eliot recorded in her journal:

...as usual, I am suffering much from doubt as to the worth of what I am
doing, and fear lest I may not be able to complete it so as to make it
a contribution to literature, and not a mere addition to the heap of
books. I am now just beginning the part about *Deronda* at page 234.[2]

This is the first mention of the novel in Cross's *Life* and
presumably she had begun to write it not long before. The book
affords a particularly clear instance of a work springing from two
different kinds of source. The conception of Gwendolen's
character and story develops out of a particular 'emotion,
recollected in tranquillity'. The conception of Daniel's character
and story arises out of a conscious—almost a propagandist—
intention. One is tempted to assert that the part of the book
concerning Gwendolen is a success and the part concerning
Daniel a failure. The tendency to dissect the novel in this way
developed early and she herself protested against it. She wrote
to Madame Bodichon on 2 October 1876:

I have had some very interesting letters both from Jews and from
Christians about *Deronda*. Part of the scene at the club is translated
into Hebrew in a German-Jewish newspaper. On the other hand,
a Christian (highly accomplished) thanks me for embodying the
principles by which Christ wrought and will conquer. This is better

[1] *Daniel Deronda*, ch. I.   [2] Cross, vol. III, p. 251.

than the laudation of readers who cut the book up into scraps, and talk of nothing in it but Gwendolen. I meant everything in the book to be related to everything else there.[1]

As regards the contrivance of the plot and the invention of a pattern of events in which the main characters affect one another, everything in the novel is successfully related to everything else. And, as regards the two central themes, the development of Gwendolen's character and Deronda's discovery of his mission, some connection is also achieved. The reader cannot fully discover Gwendolen's character or Deronda's without taking into account the relationship that develops between them. Deronda is attracted by her at the gaming-table and she is impressed by his intervention when he redeems the necklace she has pawned. The initial emotional disturbance each causes in the other develops by the end of the novel into passionate possessive love on her side and romantic, altruistic devotion on his. It is in a sense therefore impossible to 'cut the book up into scraps' without describing it falsely, since the author has arranged that the two main themes shall be intertwined. But this is a deliberate contrivance of her craftsmanship rather than a necessary consequence of her response to her subject. There is no inevitable connection between the perception of Gwendolen's predicament and of Deronda's as there is between Lydgate's and Dorothea's. The widely separate origins of the two themes, separate in kind as well as in time, create a fissure between them of which most readers have been conscious in spite of the bridges the author has built across it. Whereas Gwendolen is the product of an impulse of pity, an emotion experienced in 1872 and recollected in 1875, Deronda is to some extent the product of a conscientious determination to arouse sympathy for the Jews. In October 1876, George Eliot wrote to Harriet Beecher Stowe (author of *Uncle Tom's Cabin*):

As to the Jewish element in *Deronda*, I expected from first to last in writing it, that it would create much stronger resistance, and even

[1] Cross, vol. III p. 290.

repulsion than it has actually met with. But precisely because I felt that the usual attitude of Christians towards Jews is—I hardly know whether to say more impious or more stupid, when viewed in the light of their professed principles, I therefore felt urged to treat Jews with such sympathy and understanding as my nature and knowledge could attain to. Moreover, not only towards the Jews, but towards all Oriental peoples with whom we English come into contact, a spirit of arrogance and contemptuous dictatorialness is observable which has become a national disgrace to us. There is nothing I should care more to do, if it were possible, than to rouse the imagination of men and women to a vision of human claims in those races of their fellow-men who most differ from them in customs and beliefs. But towards the Hebrews we western people, who have been reared in Christianity, have a peculiar debt, and, whether we acknowledge it or not, a peculiar thoroughness of fellowship in religious and moral sentiment. Can anything be more disgusting than to hear people called 'educated' making small jokes about eating ham, and showing themselves empty of any real knowledge as to the relation of their own social and religious life to the history of the people they think themselves witty in insulting? They hardly know that Christ was a Jew. And I find men, educated, supposing that Christ spoke Greek. To my feeling, this deadness to the history which has prepared half our world for us, this inability to find interest in any form of life that is not clad in the same coat-tails and flounces as our own, lies very close to the worst kind of irreligion. The best that can be said of it is, that it is a sign of the intellectual narrowness—in plain English, the stupidity—which is still the average mark of our culture.[1]

The good sense and good feeling that actuated George Eliot in composing her last novel were in some degree hostile to her creative power. In this book, as in *Romola*, there is too much deliberate intention, and it leads her too far from the scenes with which she had been familiar in her youth and in which her imagination is most at home. As with *Romola* she prepared herself to write the book by a course of serious study, this time of Jewish history and Jewish thought. The favourable impression the book made on learned Jews in her own time bears witness to

[1] Cross, vol. III, p. 295.

the thoroughness of her researches. But the language of Mordecai has the same kind of unreality and produces the same sense of being thought out rather than heard as that of her educated Florentines. In his first explanation of his hopes to Deronda, Mordecai says:

'I speak not as an ignorant dreamer—as one bred up in the inland valleys, thinking ancient thoughts anew and not knowing them ancient, never having stood by the great waters where the world's knowledge passes to and fro. English is my mother-tongue, England is the native land of this body, which is but as a breaking pot of earth around the fruit-bearing tree, whose seed might make the desert rejoice....'[1]

And the reader is not convinced that English is his mother tongue, because he speaks in rhythms that no one hears, unless from a Nonconformist pulpit, and uses images from Hebrew literature which makes his language not only foreign but self-conscious. It is not that George Eliot had lost her ear for dialogue, but that she was conscientiously constructing Mordecai's speech instead of hearing it. The little cockney Jew, Cohen, speaks convincingly and the images he uses are those of his class and type. He endears himself to the reader with his racy and characteristic talk, whereas Mordecai leaves the reader, at best, unmoved and unconvinced by his self-conscious speeches or, at worst, irritated by his prophetic posturing.

Intellect and conscience usurp the place of creative power over an area of the novel which lies at the centre of the author's intention in it. The character of Daniel himself, as well as of Mordecai and all the mechanism of the plot that concerns Daniel's discovery of his vocation, falls within that area. The unconvincing idiom in which Mordecai speaks is only one symptom of the failure of creative power. The improbabilities of the plot and the failure to sustain the illusion of inevitability in its development are other symptoms. It soon becomes obvious that Daniel is to discover some important relation between himself and Mordecai and that Mordecai is to find in him the fulfilment of his prophetic

[1] *Daniel Deronda*, bk. v, ch. XL.

dreams. In order to bring this about the reader must first accept the accident that Daniel finds himself at precisely the right place at the right time to prevent Mirah's suicide; then that the name Ezra Cohen over a shop leads him to the discovery of her lost brother, although that brother is not related to the Ezra Cohen there designated; then that this brother, Mordecai, has long been waiting for a man of Deronda's type, but one who must be a Jew, who will fulfil the mission Mordecai himself is too ill to carry through; then that Daniel, who has been thirsting for precisely some such mission is, though he does not know it, Jewish-born; and finally, that his Jewish mother, who has hitherto contrived that he shall know nothing of his origins, chooses the exact moment that the story requires to send for him and reveal his Jewish birth. If all this is accepted as a romantic legend symbolizing the author's moral idea (that men are tied by innate bonds of sympathy to the traditions of their race) a yet graver obstacle to our 'willing suspension of disbelief' supervenes. If the reader is to respond to the Jewish theme in the novel in the way the author intends he must not only accept this curious concatenation of circumstances, he must also welcome the solution of Daniel's personal problem that they are supposed to provide. His problem, like Dorothea's, is to find in the modern world an employment to satisfy his aspiration to serve mankind. And George Eliot several times in the novel uses a character as the mouthpiece of an argument intended to win sympathy for the vocation Daniel discovers through Mordecai. The Zionist Movement was founded in 1900, twenty-four years after the novel was published. George Eliot knew nothing, and apparently foresaw nothing, of the international problems that would follow in its train. The claims of the Arabs in Palestine did not enter her head. She believed that the Jewish race, and every race, had a special contribution to make to the progress of mankind. She thought that the contribution of the Jews could best be made by the rebirth of Jewish national consciousness which would be fostered by a return of some section of the Jewish people to Palestine, there to found and develop a Jewish state. Such is the policy which Mordecai is made to advocate and Deronda to accept. Mordecai states his case, with characteristic afflatus, at the working men's discussion club:

'Revive the organic centre: let the unity of Israel which has made the growth and form of its religion be an outward reality. Looking towards a land and a polity, our dispersed people in all the ends of the earth may share the dignity of a national life which has a voice among the peoples of the East and the West—which will plant the wisdom and skill of our race so that it may be, as of old, a medium of transmission and understanding. Let that come to pass, and the living warmth will spread to the weak extremities of Israel, and superstition will vanish, not in the lawlessness of the renegade, but in the illumination of great facts which widen feeling, and make all knowledge alive as the young offspring of beloved memories.'

A little more soberly and clearly George Eliot's doctrine is expounded by Kalonymos when he explains Daniel's grandfather's views to him:

'What he used to insist on was that the strength and wealth of mankind depended on the balance of separateness and communication, and he was bitterly against our people losing themselves among the Gentiles; "It's no better", said he, "than the many sorts of grain going back from their variety into sameness".'[2]

And Deronda himself, when he has assimilated the ideas he is to propagate, explains them to Gwendolen and makes the nature of his mission yet more precise and, thereby, more controversial:

'The idea that I am possessed with is that of restoring a political existence to my people, making them a nation again, giving them a national centre, such as the English have, though they too are scattered over the face of the globe.'[3]

The accident that this scheme for a national Jewish home in Palestine has become a desperately difficult political issue serves to emphasize the danger of incorporating propaganda in a fiction. No modern reader can accept Deronda's mission unquestioningly as a valuable service to mankind, but to George Eliot herself it seemed to offer a more promising field than politics for his altruistic

---

[1] *Daniel Deronda*, bk. VI, ch. XLII. [2] Ibid., bk. VIII, ch. LX.
[3] Ibid., bk. VIII, ch. LXIX.

energies. There are indications in *Felix Holt*, in *Middlemarch* and elsewhere in *Daniel Deronda* that the field of English politics seemed to her unsuitable for a man of integrity. Presumably the disappointing results of the Reform Bills had disillusioned her as it had many of her contemporaries. At the close of *Middlemarch* she explains that though Will Ladislaw himself

became an ardent public man, working well in those times when reforms were begun with a young hopefulness of immediate good which has been much checked in our days,

his son

who might have represented Middlemarch...declined thinking that his opinions had less chance of being stifled if he remained out of doors.[1]

Similarly, Daniel Deronda when, before he comes under Mordecai's influence, he is 'occupied with uncertainties about his own course' perceives

the strong array of reasons why he should shrink from getting into that routine of the world which makes men apologise for all its wrong-doing, and take opinions as mere professional equipment—why he should not draw strongly at any thread in the hopelessly entangled scheme of things.[2]

To her the creation of a Jewish national home in Palestine seemed a non-political, non-controversial cause for her hero to embrace. But when she became the advocate of a cause she deserted her own vocation and spoilt her novel. She herself had written to Frederic Harrison on 15 August 1866:

I think aesthetic teaching is the highest of all teaching, because it deals with life in its highest complexity. But if it ceases to be purely aesthetic—if it lapses anywhere from the picture to the diagram—it becomes the most offensive of all teaching.[3]

In her presentation of Daniel Deronda, of Mordecai and of Mirah, George Eliot is not dealing 'with life in its highest complexity'. She over-simplifies these three characters because she uses them to illustrate a preconceived idea. She is not

[1] *Middlemarch*, bk. VIII, ch. LXXXVI.   [2] *Daniel Deronda*, bk. II, ch. XVII.
[3] Cross, vol. II, p. 441.

primarily interested in them as human beings. They are the product of her conscious conception of ideal personality. Consequently, they do not convince nor even delight the reader; their speeches are guardedly composed so as not to admit any selfish or cowardly or commonplace thought. It is not that we do not prefer people to be without such flaws, nor that we do not believe that some people are neither selfish, nor cowardly, nor commonplace. But, because George Eliot is composing from the head and giving too little rein to her imagination, her own self-consciousness about these characters translates itself into the semblance of self-righteousness in them. They appear to be deliberately rather than instinctively good and they fail to please for the same reason as Dinah Morris often fails to please in *Adam Bede*.

But George Eliot does not altogether fail in her attempt to win sympathy for the Jews. That compassionate motive is not identical with the will to state a case for Zionism. Though Daniel, Mordecai and Mirah fail to affect the reader as they were meant to do, other Jews in the novel are more convincing; the musician Klesmer, for instance (one of the rare examples of genius successfully suggested in fiction), or the vulgar, mercenary, affectionate Cohen family, or Daniel's mother (though she is only sketched in) who repudiated the restricting claims of race and religion to follow her own taste and talent as an opera-singer, and who tried in vain to protect her son from the claims of Judaism, or the clever, cringing, rootless ne'er-do-well who is the father of Mirah and Mordecai. George Eliot has discovered the variety of intellectual and moral range among these Jews, and has shown in each of them, along with the well-observed insignia of race, the endearing imperfections of our common humanity.

Moreover, in spite of the central flaw in it, George Eliot's last novel is in some parts as interesting as any she ever wrote, both intrinsically and in relation to the developing art of fiction. For her way of presenting some of the characters in this novel is in some respects different from any she or her predecessors had used before. This is particularly noticeable in the way in which

Gwendolen's character is gradually revealed and developed, but the surprisingly successful portrait of Grandcourt (*surprisingly* because he belongs to a class and a moral type with which George Eliot can have had no intimate contact) is also due to an advance in technique, and that advance is itself the result of a more complex vision. In the structure of the novel Grandcourt is important solely in his relation to Gwendolen. The increased mastery of method shows itself in the absence of any serious attempt to make him known to the reader except in that relation. There are no explanations of his moral nature comparable with those about Tito Melema in *Romola*. In sharp contrast to the attempt there made to give a complete account of a vicious nature here the limitations of knowledge are emphasized:

> Attempts at description are stupid: who can all at once describe a human being? even when he is presented to us we only begin that knowledge of his appearance which must be completed by innumerable impressions under differing circumstances. We recognise the alphabet; we are not sure of the language. I am only mentioning the points that Gwendolen saw by the light of a prepared contrast in the first minutes of her meeting with Grandcourt: they were summed up in the words, 'He is not ridiculous'.[1]

In the scene that follows between them, at an archery meeting at which they have been first introduced to one another, George Eliot indicates the stream of Gwendolen's consciousness as it flows on beneath the conversation between them. Their talk is polite and superficial, a pretended attempt to get to know one another by talking lightly about tastes and pastimes. Grandcourt's talk is mainly of his boredom with all the pleasures of a wealthy and idle life. Gwendolen, though she is younger, less experienced and relatively poor, is suffering from the same malady. But while they talk of archery and hunting she is thinking of the impression she is making on him and of what it would be like to be the wife of such a man. The technique is a little clumsy; the conversation is interrupted by parentheses that record her thoughts:

[1] *Daniel Deronda*, bk. II, ch. XI.

(Pause, during which she imagined various degrees and modes of opinion about herself that might be entertained by Grandcourt)

or, a little later:

(Pause, during which Gwendolen thought that a man of extremely calm, cold manners might be less disagreeable as a husband than other men, and not likely to interfere with his wife's preferences.)

But, though modern writers have developed techniques that produce the required effect more economically and more subtly, the recognition that such reflections as these often accompany a conversation that reveals nothing of them, implies a more complex conception of character-drawing than was usual in Victorian fiction. The portrait of Gwendolen, if it was to succeed as it undoubtedly does, required more subtlety from the author than did the portrait of Maggie or of Dorothea. Not only are those relatively single-minded characters simpler in themselves than the unregenerate Gwendolen, but they are also much more like their author. Introspection cannot have helped her very much in understanding Gwendolen. A greater effort of self-projection was required than for any former study of comparable thoroughness, except that of Mrs Transome, and about her we know very much less than about Gwendolen. Maggie and Dorothea both pass, as George Eliot herself did, through a period of fervent religious belief which bore fruit in extreme self-abnegation at the time and left a permanent trace on their mind and feelings. Gwendolen's experience was widely different; she had

always disliked whatever was presented to her under the name of religion, in the same way that some people dislike arithmetic and accounts: it had raised no other emotion in her, no alarm, no longing; so that the question whether she believed it had not occurred to her, any more than it had occurred to her to inquire into the conditions of colonial property and banking, on which, as she had had many opportunities of knowing, the family fortune was dependent.[1]

Similarly, Maggie and Dorothea were, like their author, impulsive and affectionate; they were also passionate and prone

[1] Ibid., bk. I, ch. VI.

to fall in love. In Gwendolen, on the contrary, George Eliot set herself to imagine the feelings of a girl whose nature is cold and who recoils instinctively from intimacy with men. The whole episode with Rex, and the reaction from it which hastens her into marriage with Grandcourt, illustrates with what sureness she achieved this. Gwendolen's outward behaviour to her young cousin is that of an ordinary coquette, she encourages him without caring for him; his attentions flatter her and amuse her. But her inner feelings are more complicated than that:

> Gwendolen was perfectly aware that her cousin was in love with her; but she had no idea that the matter was of any consequence, having never had the slightest visitation of painful love herself. She wished the small romance of Rex's devotion to fill up the time of his stay at Pennicote, and to avoid explanations which would bring it to an untimely end. Besides, she objected, with a sort of physical repulsion, to being directly made love to.[1]

She is not skilled enough to fend off the proposal and when it comes about she is frightened and horrified:

> Gwendolen herself could not have foreseen that she should feel in this way. It was all a sudden, new experience to her. The day before she had been quite aware that her cousin was in love with her—she did not mind how much, so that he said nothing about it; and if any one had asked her why she objected to love-making speeches, she would have said laughingly, 'Oh, I am tired of them all in the books'. But now the life of passion had begun negatively in her. She felt passionately averse to this volunteered love.[2]

When she has dismissed her lover and seen his distress she is despairingly unhappy, not so much because of the pain she has given, though that too makes her uncomfortable, but because of what she has discovered in herself:

> 'I shall never love anybody. I can't love people. I hate them.'

She says to her mother: 'I can't bear any one to be very near me but you.' There is almost a whole volume of the novel between this

---

[1] *Daniel Deronda*, bk. I, ch. VII.   [2] Ibid.

scene and Grandcourt's proposal but the two scenes complement one another and together show how completely George Eliot was able to understand and to portray this aspect of Gwendolen's character. She is persuaded to accept Grandcourt's proposal almost as much by the coldness of his manners as by the prospect of relief from poverty and a future of affluence and elegance. It is the absence in his proposal of any expression of strong feeling that tips the balance in his favour:

> She had a momentary phantasmal love for this man who chose his words so well, and who was a mere incarnation of delicate homage.[1]

She accepts him although she knows he has two children by another woman to whom he has long promised marriage. To deaden her conscience scruples she persuades herself that her dominant motive is altruistic, she is marrying for the sake of her mother and when that plaintive but long-suffering woman said:

> 'My dear child, I trust you are not going to marry only for my sake.' ... Gwendolen tossed her head on the pillow away from her mother, and let the ring lie. She was irritated at this attempt to take away a motive.[2]

Throughout the novel George Eliot sustains this subtle insight into Gwendolen's character and reveals alongside her actions and her speech the underlying motives of which Gwendolen herself is only partly conscious. At the climax, in the boat on the Italian lake, Gwendolen is herself uncertain how far her consenting will makes her responsible for Grandcourt's death. The situation is comparable to that which T. S. Eliot treats in his poetic drama *The Family Reunion*. In her account of the event to Deronda Gwendolen says:[3]

> 'I don't know how it was—he was turning the sail—there was a gust—he was struck—I know nothing—I only know that I saw my wish outside me.'

[1] Ibid., bk. III, ch. XXVII. [2] Ibid., bk. IV, ch. XXVIII.
[3] Ibid., bk. VII, ch. LVI.

She describes what she actually did to save him from drowning and how her actions were accompanied by the wish that he might drown:

'...and my heart said, "Die!"—and he sank; and I felt "It is done—I am wicked, I am lost!"—and I had the rope in my hand—I don't know what I thought—I was leaping away from myself—I would have saved him then. I was leaping from my crime, and there it was—close to me as I fell—there was the dead face—dead, dead. It can never be altered. That was what happened. That was what I did. You know it all. It can never be altered.'[1]

'It can never be altered'—that is a theme that runs through all George Eliot's novels, 'what's done cannot be undone', but nowhere else has she raised the problem of responsibility in this deeply perplexing form.

Wherever in this novel George Eliot escapes from the conscious intention to illustrate an idea and devotes herself to the discovery of the personalities she has selected for her drama there is evidence of this increased insight into the complexity of human motives. Daniel Deronda himself in his relation to Gwendolen ceases to be merely the incarnation of an idea. She perceives the interplay of ordinary human impulses with the dominant altruistic bias that shapes his character. From the beginning of Daniel's intercourse with Gwendolen he is drawn to her as much by the magnetism which an attractive girl has for a normal man as by the appeal her plight makes to his chivalry:

Persons attracted him, as Hans Meyrick had done, in proportion to the possibility of his defending them, rescuing them, telling upon their lives with some sort of redeeming influence; and he had to resist an inclination, easily accounted for, to withdraw coldly from the fortunate. But in the movement which had led him to redeem Gwendolen's necklace for her, and which was at work in him still, there was something beyond his habitual compassionate fervour—something due to the fascination of her womanhood.[2]

When he meets her again after her marriage with Grandcourt there is the same double appeal; she is obviously unhappy, she is

[1] *Daniel Deronda*, bk. VII, ch. LVI. [2] Ibid., bk. IV, ch. XXVIII.

equally obviously fascinating. His own feelings about her are almost as enigmatic to him as are Grandcourt's; he becomes uncomfortably aware of cross currents of feeling in relation to them both:

Was he going to be a jealous husband? Deronda imagined that to be likely; but his imagination was as much astray about Grandcourt as it would have been about an unexplored continent where all the species were peculiar. He did not conceive that he himself was a likely object of jealousy, or that he should give any pretext for it; but the suspicion that a wife is not happy naturally leads one to speculate on the husband's private deportment; and Deronda found himself after one o'clock in the morning in the rather ludicrous position of sitting up severely holding a Hebrew grammar in his hands (for somehow, in deference to Mordecai, he had begun to study Hebrew), with the consciousness that he had been in that attitude nearly an hour, and had thought of nothing but Gwendolen and her husband. To be an unusual young man means for the most part to get a difficult mastery over the usual, which is often like the sprite of ill-luck you pack up your goods to escape from, and see grinning at you from the top of your luggage-van.[1]

If the ironic eye that George Eliot here turns upon her hero had been active throughout the novel he would have been as convincing and sympathetic to the reader as Gwendolen, and the vitality that informs one part of the book might have extended to the whole. But this kind of irony (composite of amusement and compassion) vanishes when her attention is distracted. She cannot achieve it when she uses her characters to illustrate ideas 'lapsing from the picture to the diagram', but only when she looks undisturbedly at 'life in its highest complexity'.

George Eliot was keenly aware of this distinction between art and propaganda (the quotation is from her letter to Frederic Harrison, 15 August 1866); but her unusual combination of gifts made it especially difficult for her to avoid occasional lapses. Her intellect was active and well-informed, that is an important part of her strength. But, as many writers have stated, creative art demands that the mind be passive; it is the

[1] Ibid., bk. v, ch. xxxv.

fruit of contemplation: 'Ce n'est pas par l'esprit que l'on crée,...
l'esprit au contraire s'entend à merveille à empêcher la création.'[1]
George Eliot herself told Cross that in all her best work there
was a '"not herself" which took possession of her, and that
she felt her own personality to be merely the instrument through
which this spirit, as it were, was acting'.[2] She could not do her
best work when a premeditated intention intervened between
her and the direct vision of her subject, and the reader is occasion-
ally aware of such a rift between the thinker and the artist.
The too-conscious activity of her mind accounts for the brilliant,
but cold, analysis of Tito's character, while, in *Daniel Deronda*,
it accounts for a radical mistake in the structure of the novel.
On the other hand her intellectual strength is an asset; when
her mind is passive in the act of creation, her vision of life bears
the imprint of her previous mental activity. It is the intelligence
illuminating her compassion that makes her more fully aware
of the complexities of human life than are any of her contemporaries. But, in consequence, the traditional novel-form,
with its wide and crowded canvas, is unsuited to some aspects
of her vision. Her conception of Maggie's moral problem, or of
Mrs Transome's or Gwendolen's nature, needed the spacious
treatment that Henry James or Conrad ensured for themselves
by limiting the interest of a long novel to the development of
a single human situation. Thus, besides being the greatest
English novelist in her own time, George Eliot points forward
to subsequent developments in the art of fiction.

[1] Charles du Bos, *Journal*, p. 25.   [2] Cross, vol. III, p. 424.

LIST OF THE BOOKS REFERRED TO IN THE TEXT

ACTON, LORD. *Historical Essays and Studies.* 1907.

BETHELL, S. *The Criterion.* 1938.

BLIND, M. *George Eliot.* 1883.

BOURL'HONNE, P. *George Eliot: Essai de Biographie intellectuelle et morale, 1819–1854.* Paris, 1933.

BRAY, C. *Phases of Opinion and Experience during a Long Life.* 1884.

COMTE, A. *The Positive Philosophy,* translated by H. Martineau. 1853.

—— *Comte's Philosophy of the Sciences,* translated by G. H. Lewes. 1853.

CROSS, J. W. *George Eliot's Life as related in her Letters and Journals. Arranged and edited by her Husband, J. W. Cross.* 1885.

ESPINASSE, F. *Literary Recollections and Sketches.* 1893.

HAIGHT, G. S. *George Eliot and John Chapman.* 1940.

HENNELL, C. C. *An Inquiry concerning the Origin of Christianity.* 1838.

HUTTON, R. H. *Essays on some of the Modern Guides of English Thought.* 1887.

—— *Essays, Theological and Literary.* 1871.

JAMES, H. *The Middle Years.* 1917.

—— *Partial Portraits.* 1888.

KITCHEL, A. T. *George Lewes and George Eliot.* New York, 1933.

LAYARD, G. S. *Mrs Lynn Linton. Her Life, Letters and Opinions.* 1901.

LEAVIS, F. R. *Scrutiny.* 1945–6.

LEWES, G. H. *On Actors and the Art of Acting.* 1875.

—— *Biographical History of Philosophy.* 4 vols. 1845–6.

—— *The Life and Works of Goethe.* 2 vols. 1855.

—— *Comte's Philosophy of the Sciences.* 1853.

—— *Problems of Life and Mind.* 5 vols. 1874–9.

LEWES, G. H. and FOSTER, J. *Dramatic Essays,* ed. by W. Archer and R. W. Lowe. 1896.

LINTON, E. L. *My Literary Life in London.* 1899.

LOCKER-LAMPSON, F. *My Confidences.* 1896.

SPENCER, H. *Autobiography.* 1904.

LIST OF BOOKS REFERRED TO IN TEXT

SPINOZA, B. DE. *Ethics.* 1677.
———   *Tractatus Theologico-Politicus.* 1670.
TAYLOR, I. *Ancient Christianity and The Oxford Tracts.* 1839–42.
Temple Bar. 1885.
WEBB, BEATRICE. *My Apprenticeship.* 1926.
WOOLF, V. *The Common Reader.* First Series. 1925.
YEATS, WILLIAM BUTLER. *Ideas of Good and Evil.* 1903.

INDEX

INDEX

INDEX

Monna Lisa, 143

Mordecai, 58, 90, 91, 145, 185, 186–9

More, Hannah, 7

Morris, Dinah, 11, 96, 102–5, 107–9, 111–12, 189

Moss, Mrs, 82

Mr Gilfil's Love Story, 73, 98; *and see Scenes of Clerical Life*

Munich, 104

'My Aunt's Story', 103; *and see Adam Bede*

Myshkin, Prince, Dostoyevski's, 108, 109

Nello, 142, 143

Newman, John Henry, 14, 15, 148, 149

Noble, Miss, 174, 176

Olding, John, 95

Owen, Robert, 34

Oxford Movement, The, 10, 12

Oxford Tracts, The, 12–15

Patten, Mrs, 86

Pears, Mrs, 19, 30, 34, 39

Pollock, Frederick, *Spinoza, his Life and Philosophy*, 41

Poyser, Mrs, 86, 108, 179

Poysers, the, 79–80, 89

Proust, Marcel, *Du Coté de chez Swann*, 115, 141, 142

Pullet, Lucy, 117–19, 127

Pullet, Mrs, 81

Raffles, 98, 99, 170, 171

Red Lion Square, Holborn, 57, 58

Rochester, Mr, 121, 122, 125; *and see Eyre, Jane*

Romola, 4, 96, 97, 144, 145, 150

Romola, 43, 78, 79, 83, 139–51, 152, 153, 160, 179, 184

Rosehill, Coventry, 46

Rousseau, Jean Jacques, 27

Ruskin, John, *Fiction Fair and Foul*, 116 n.

Sand, George, 27

Savonarola, 139, 145, 148–50

Scenes of Clerical Life, 43, 71, 73, 78, 82, 92, 97, 99, 103

Sibree, John, 26, 35

Sibree, Mary, 34, 35

Sibree, Mrs John, 7

Sibrees, the, 33

Silas Marner, 43, 82, 131–8, 139, 141

Smith, George, 140

Smith, Harriet, 119

Sorley, William Ritchie, 59

Sorrel, Hetty, 79–80, 94–7, 104–6, 110, 112, 161

Spencer, Herbert, 25, 26, 45, 48, 49–53, 60, 62, 65, 67

    Autobiography, 49–53

    Social Statics, 53, 60

Spinoza, 40–3, 57–61

    Ethics, 41, 42

    Tractatus Theologico-Politicus, 40–2

Stephen, Sir Leslie, 56, 61

Stone, Sarah, 95

Stowe, Harriet Beecher, 183

Strauss, David Frederick, *Leben Jesu*, 5, 35–7, 40, 41

Taylor, Isaac, 13–18

    Ancient Christianity and the Oxford Tracts, 13–18, 20

Temple Bar (1885), 45, 48, 66

Tessa, 96, 143, 145, 146

Thackeray, William Makepeace, 105, 106

    Vanity Fair, 105, 106

The Lifted Veil, 115

Tilley, Elisabeth, 45–7, 49

Timoleon, poem on, 161

Tolstoi, Leo, *War and Peace*, 151

Transome, Harold, 154, 156, 158

Transome, Mrs, 44, 83, 97, 153, 157, 159

Trollope, Anthony, *Can You Forgive Her?*, 129

Trounsem, Tom, 155

Tryan, Mr, 145

Tulliver, Maggie, 4, 5, 6, 7, 16, 31, 39, 44, 65, 81–3, 115–17, 119–20, 123–30, 133, 144, 161, 191

Tulliver, Mr, 5, 81, 82, 115

202

INDEX